BASIC GARDENING
Illustrated

By the Editors of Sunset Books and Sunset Magazine

Lane Publishing Co., Menlo Park, California

Foreword

Gardening is the oldest civilized activity of humankind, and it is still one of the most rewarding and least complicated. But even though this universal pastime is pleasant and simple once you know what you're doing, a helping hand or bit of advice at the start can save disappointment.

If you've never turned a spadeful of earth (or even if you've gardened for years by rule of thumb), the early sections of this book will help you to understand the soil underfoot: what it's composed of, how to improve it, how to water it and add nutrients for good plant growth.

Once you've dealt, literally, with the groundwork, you can delve into special techniques such as sowing seeds, growing cuttings, and making grafts. You can learn how to be a wise nursery shopper, and how to get your plant off to a good start after you bring it home.

Later pages cover such specialties as outdoor gardening in containers, indoor plants, vegetable gardening, flowering plants, and basic trees and shrubs. A special section at the end interprets some of the special gardening jargon that old hands like to toss around in conversation.

Here, then, is a reference book to garden fundamentals. You'll find it comes in handy from the day you choose your first spade to the time later on when you may decide to try your hand at something like T-budding or the use of coldframes.

Research and Text: Will Kirkman

Special Consultant: Joseph F. Williamson
Garden Editor, Sunset Magazine
Coordinating Editor: Sherry Gellner
Design and Illustration: Joe Seney, E. D. Bills
Cover: Photograph by Ells Marugg

Editor, Sunset Books: David E. Clark

Contents

SOIL
...the first of all the basics

In some gardens the soil is like glue when it's wet and like brick when it's dry. In others you can pour on water until the bill reaches three figures and still find some plants drying up. But even if that first spadeful of soil looks as if it wouldn't grow weeds, there's no reason to be discouraged. With a little time and effort you can solve almost any soil problem.

The first step is to find out what type of soil you have. Read the descriptions of soil types below and compare them with your own soil. If it needs improvement, check over the chart of soil amendments on pages 6 and 7. The important thing to keep in mind is that any soil problem has some kind of solution. After all, you can garden on concrete if you use containers and a good potting mix.

Finally, don't be impatient. It may take several seasons of doctoring to achieve a permanent change in soil quality. In the interim, a wise choice of plants and regular watering and fertilizing can give heartening results.

SOIL TYPES

Heavy soil. Called either clay or adobe, heavy soil is easy to recognize but hard to work with. When it's wet it sticks to your spade. Squeeze a handful together and you'll get a gummy plastic mass that doesn't break apart even if you tap it with your shovel. When heavy soil dries, it tends to crack, and often becomes hard enough to deflect a pick. Individual particles of clay are very fine. With a microscope you would see them as flat plates. Because of their shape, they pack tightly together. One large particle is just 1/25 the size of the smallest grain of sand. There's no air in soil like this, and drainage is poor. Plant roots will refuse to grow because of the lack of air and often drown because of the lack of drainage.

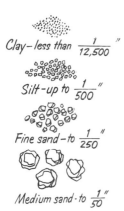

Clay – less than $\frac{1}{12,500}$"

Silt – up to $\frac{1}{500}$"

Fine sand – to $\frac{1}{250}$"

Medium sand – to $\frac{1}{50}$"

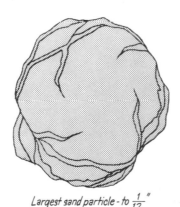

Largest sand particle – to $\frac{1}{12}$"

You can improve heavy soil by adding an organic amendment, such as compost, peat moss, or leaf mold. Mixed in thoroughly, these materials immediately create countless tiny air pockets between the flat plates of clay. As they continue to decay, a material called "humus" forms, preventing the clay particles from packing down again.

The advantage of heavy soil is that the clay particles tend to retain moisture and fertilizer. And if you improve it by adding an amendment, heavy soil pays you back by making every drop of water and every ounce of plant food count.

Sandy soil. At its worst, sandy soil is the exact opposite of clay. No matter how often you wet it, the big rounded particles quickly dry up.

There's plenty of air in soil like this, and roots can go where they like. But water pours right through, taking with it any plant food you've added.

Sandy soil can also be improved by adding organic amendments. The amendment particles fill the open spaces between sand particles and help to retain water and nutrients. As an amendment decays, however, the resulting humus tends to leach away with each watering. That won't happen right away, but if, after a few seasons, you seem to be watering more than usual, give your soil another application of the organic amendment.

SOIL AMENDMENTS

Soil amendments are of two distinctly different types. The first type may be almost anything that comes originally from an animal or plant (bone meal, peat moss, or manure). Some of these amendments are primarily a source of nutrients and are normally used as fertilizer. An example is bone meal which is rich in phosphorus. Others have no nutrients but help fluff up heavy soil and then rot to produce humus (peat moss is of this type). Some contain tiny amounts of plant nutrients (manure is an example) but are used mainly as soil improvers.

The second type of amendment is purely mineral. It comes in small-chunk form. Added to fine, heavy soil, it stays in place more or less permanently. Some examples are sand, perlite, pumice, and vermiculite. Most of these materials are too expensive for large areas but are often used in special soil mixtures for containers.

Texture is important. In choosing an amendment, the most important consideration is texture. In the chart on pages 6 and 7, texture is described in the column, "Pros and Cons." If possible, choose an amendment that is granular and fine-grained. Granular materials are easier than fibrous materials to mix evenly into the soil. And, in general, even-textured materials amend the soil better than highly variable ones. For example, sawdust that has a high percentage of large shavings and wood chips is less effective than the same kind of sawdust that is composed of tiny particles.

Check for salt content. If you live in an area with a normal amount of rainfall, some salt content in soil amendments will cause little if any trouble. But if you live in a region with low rainfall, the salt content is crucial. Manures often contain quantities of salts. Without heavy rains to wash away these salts, you may find that young or sensitive plants begin to show burned leaf edges.

What about nitrogen? Materials such as sawdust, ground bark, and straw quickly decompose after you mix them with soil. The rotting agents are fungus and bacteria. As they work to break down the amendment, they use up nitrogen. Unless you add nitrogen to the soil along with the conditioner, your plants will not have enough nitrogen for growth. You may use either a chemical fertilizer, such as ammonium nitrate, or an organic fertilizer, such as blood meal. The chemical fertilizers may burn plants when used in large quantities, so the organics are safer as a rule.

The chart on pages 6 and 7 gives the amount of nitrogen you should add to your amendment in number of actual pounds. If you choose a chemical fertilizer, the package label tells you only the *percentage* of nitrogen it contains, so you'll have to translate the first number on the package of fertilizer into **actual** pounds of nitrogen. Look for a group of three numbers on the label, something like 10-8-6. From left to right, these numbers give the percentage of nitrogen, phosphorus, and potassium in the material. The hypothetical 10-8-6 fertilizer

contains 10 percent nitrogen compounds, 8 percent of a phosphorus compound, 6 percent of a potassium compound, and 76 percent inert material. If you use raw redwood sawdust you'll need to add ⅓ pound **actual** nitrogen for each 10 cubic feet of sawdust you add to the soil. If you have a 25 pound bag of a fertilizer labeled 10-8-6, you would calculate that 10 percent of 25 pounds is 2.5. This means that the bag of fertilizer contains 2.5 pounds of actual nitrogen. Since you need to add ⅓ pound of nitrogen, you will use roughly 1/7 of the fertilizer. You don't have to be absolutely exact. Just visually divide the bag into seven parts and scoop out what you need.

If you use bloodmeal or hoof-and-horn meal ("organic fertilizer" on the soil amendment chart) no figuring is necessary. Use the amount stated on the chart.

How much is ash? Also an important consideration in choosing an organic amendment is the quantity of ash (mineral matter) it contains. Ash is of questionable value in improving soil. And the higher the percentage, the less efficient the conditioner. For example, a truckload of fine sawdust may contain from ½ to 3 percent ash. A truckload of poor quality manure may contain up to 50 percent ash. Almost every grain of the sawdust is useful as a soil improver, while half the manure is composed of salts, stable dust and dirt, gravel scooped up with the manure, or possibly just earth from the pens.

Will it hold fertilizer? The professionals use a complicated term—"cation exchange capacity"—when they are talking about whether or not the plant food you add to amended soil is going to stay there. Some materials will hold to nitrogen and other nutrients, whereas others let them slide away. Wood products are poor at holding nutrients, but that doesn't matter if the soil is heavy, since it's already a good nutrient holder. Because peat moss does the best job of conserving added nutrients, it is ideal for use in containers and sandy soils. Manure actually supplies nutrients on its own and is also good in sandy soil. However, because of its salt content, it should not be used in containers.

How much do you add? When you add an amendment, the final soil mixture should contain at least one quarter amendment and three quarters soil. But if your soil is almost pure clay or sand, the finished mix should contain about half amendment and half soil. If your spade or rotary tiller penetrates 9 inches deep (most do), you should apply a 2 to 3-inch layer of amendment over normal soil before cultivating. For a half and half mix, you'll need enough material to make a 4 to 5-inch layer. For instructions on cultivating the soil and working the amendment in evenly, see pages 12 and 13.

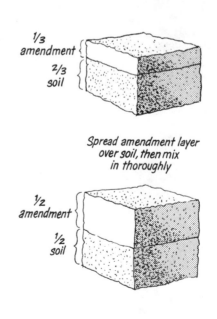

⅓ amendment
⅔ soil

Spread amendment layer over soil, then mix in thoroughly

½ amendment
½ soil

15 organic soil amendments

The materials listed in the chart below are all useful organic amendments, but their availability varies depending on where you live. Other similar products may be just as effective. However, in the listing for fir saw- dust, take special note of the warning against substituting pine sawdust. Pine breaks down rapidly, making it next to impossible for you to replace the nitrogen it uses up.

CONDITIONERS SHOWN ACTUAL SIZE	PROS AND CONS	USES	MUST YOU ADD NITROGEN?	ASH CONTENT	NUTRIENT HOLDING
REDWOOD PRODUCTS	Granular, or granular-fibrous if bark used in mix. Works in well. Low salinity, ash; long lasting in soil	Work into soil or use in container mix	Raw redwood needs ⅓ pound actual nitrogen or 2½ pounds organic fertilizer per 10 cubic feet	1 percent	Poor
BARK	Granular. Easy to mix in. Low salinity, ash. Long lasting in soil. Very dense material	Use in garden soil; in container mix; often used for orchids	Raw bark needs 1 pound actual nitrogen or 8 pounds organic fertilizer per 10 cubic feet	3-5 percent	Poor
FIR SAWDUST	Granular. Works in well. Low salinity, ash. Lasts in soil. Raw sawdust may contain chips, shavings. DO NOT USE PINE SAWDUST	In soil or containers	To raw fir sawdust add ½ pound actual nitrogen or 4 pounds organic fertilizer per 10 cubic feet	2 percent	Poor
SPHAGNUM PEAT MOSS	Fibrous or powdery. Hard to wet. Do not use dry. Low salinity, ash. Once wet, it retains water better than any other amendment	Best in container mix, but keep it damp. Good in garden soil	Needs no added nitrogen	3 percent	Very good
HYPNUM PEAT MOSS	Fibrous; texture more variable than sphagnum, but contains more nitrogen. Costs less. High ash content	In containers, fern baskets, garden soil	Needs no added nitrogen	to 30 percent	Very good
SEDGE PEAT	Fibrous; texture variable. May be saline. High ash content. May be cheaper than sphagnum	In rainy climate, use in garden soil	None needed	30-50 percent	Good
OAK LEAF MOLD	May contain leaves and twigs. Adds to soil fertility in container mix, cuts feeding a bit	In potting mix. Or sterilize, sift, and use it to start seeds	None needed. Contains other useful nutrients	to 30 percent	Good

CONDITIONERS SHOWN ACTUAL SIZE	PROS AND CONS	USES	MUST YOU ADD NITROGEN?	ASH CONTENT	NUTRIENT HOLDING
DAIRY MANURE	In some areas, may be free for the hauling. Moderately saline. High ash. Must be thoroughly decomposed. Has strong odor	Conditioner in sandy soils; as mulch	No nitrogen needed. Is a low grade fertilizer	50 percent	Good
STEER MANURE	Sold in trade-name packages. May be very highly saline. High ash. Sometimes has strong odor	Conditioner in sandy soils; as mulch	None needed. Is a low grade fertilizer	to 60 percent	Good
STABLE BEDDING	May be free from a commercial stable, but must be well composted. Mixture of straw, chips, sawdust, and animal waste. Low ash	In garden soil, as conditioner	None needed.	Low but variable depending on bedding material	Fair
COMPOST	Variable material depending on what you put in. Must be well rotted, screened. May contain disease organisms	In potting mix, mulch. Soil conditioner	Contains ample nitrogen	Variable, to 40 percent	Good
MUSHROOM COMPOST	Mostly composted horse manure. May be free near mushroom grower. Be sure it is well rotted. High ash, salinity moderate	Soil conditioner	None needed.	to 40 percent	Poor
ALMOND HULLS	Compost first because big chunks decompose slowly in soil. Only available where almonds are processed. Low ash, salinity	Garden soil conditioner	None needed. Contains potassium (potash)	to 7 percent	Poor
RICE HULLS	Easy to mix into soil. High in ash, potassium. Great loss of volume when rotted. Cheap where available	In garden soil	Add $1/5$ pound actual nitrogen or 2 pounds organic fertilizer per 10 cubic feet	30 percent	Poor
COCOA BEAN HULLS	Has good scent. Is low grade fertilizer and amendment. Low ash	In garden soil	None needed. Contains nitrogen, phosphorus, and potassium in small amounts	to 10 percent	Good

Composting is home recycling

Composting has not always been thought of as the respectable garden practice it is today. It took too much time, too much space, was too messy, and anyway, who wanted a pile of garbage in the yard?

Attitudes change. Now people are proud that they recycle organic waste instead of filling garbage cans, stuffing kitchen disposers, and calling for extra trash pickups whenever they trim a bush or two. And since smog-control laws prohibit the burning of garden trash in many areas, composting has become a convenient disposal method.

Without much preparation or expense, you can try composting to see how you like it. If you decide that it's going to be a worthwhile practice, then you'll want to construct one of the simple or complex compost bins shown on these pages. You might also consider a compost grinder. It makes the job go faster.

The section on soil improvement (pages 4–7) describes "humus," the brown or black material that forms in the ground as amendments rot. In composting, you allow this humus to form above ground, since the varied organic materials of a compost pile are easier to use once they have rotted to a uniform substance. You can compost kitchen waste, animal litter, lawn clippings, leaves, dead plants, or chopped up clippings or pruned material (avoid adding any diseased material). Anything that was once alive will do. Just pile it up in a back corner of the yard, add a handful of nitrogen fertilizer, and keep it barely moist, never wet. To add air, toss and turn the pile with a fork. Do this stirring at least once a week if you can. In varying periods of time—perhaps three weeks, perhaps twice as long—the material will rot away, becoming a dark, clean-smelling, earthy mass. The more you stir, the quicker the material will rot.

The organic process that occurs in a compost pile is simple to understand. As the material decays, fungus and bacteria grow. As they "eat" the piled waste, they produce heat, making the center of the pile very hot. If the pile is not tossed and turned to keep the heat down and let bacterial action and fungus growth continue working at high speed, many of these organisms will die, slowing down the process.

Frequent tossing and turning of the compost pile will also prevent any unpleasant odor that can result from certain bacteria working when no oxygen is present. In addition, it helps to keep down the maggots and larvae that may appear on the surface of the pile. This is especially important in warm weather when their number increases along with the number of flies.

Composting is much quicker if you only add small bits and pieces of material to the pile. Depending on the size,

Welded wire cylinder *holds compost; lift it off and set aside for easy turning, then fork mixture back in.*

a whole branch might take months or years to rot away; even a big leaf takes longer to rot than a few leaf fragments. The bacteria and fungus just can't digest hunks of material as fast as smaller pieces. You can buy machines, both gasoline and electric-powered, that chop big pieces of organic matter into bits. Some models can also be rented. And, for the rare occasion when you'll need one, city maintenance departments and tree trimming firms often have heavy duty choppers available for rental by the hour.

When your compost pile has stopped producing heat in the center and looks and smells ready for use, fork it through a frame of fine hardware cloth to sift out the big pieces. Use only the fine siftings for amending your soil and pile up the unrotted material for a second go round.

Compost grinder *chops tough material like stems and branches into small pieces that will rot quickly. Wear gloves and protect your eyes when using grinder.*

This compost bin comes apart

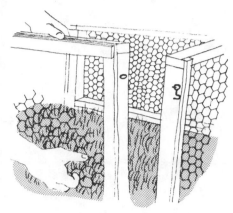

Two L-shaped frames *covered with chicken wire form simple bin. Hook and eye holds corners together. When bin is not in use, detach the two L's and place in a garage corner for space-saving storage. Sections can be any size as long as they are light enough to carry.*

A work table covers the bin

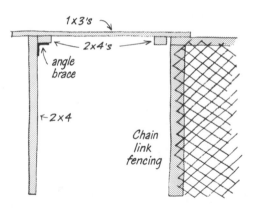

Chain link fencing *covers frame of sturdy bin. Plank cover doubles as a work table when you pull it out. Wire-sided bins allow for good air circulation and quick composting.*

Separate boxes for easy turning

Compost bin is a collection of bottomless wooden frames. Treat wood with preservatives, or use redwood or cedar in construction. Vary height of bin by removing or replacing box sections; remove one at a time to turn compost. Cover is old window screen.

Classic, but a little more costly

Three-sectioned compost bin is a classic design. The first section holds new material which you fork into second section after it rots. Sift well-rotted material from second section into third section which acts as storage bin until material can be used. Front and side boards slide out for easy turning and removing material.

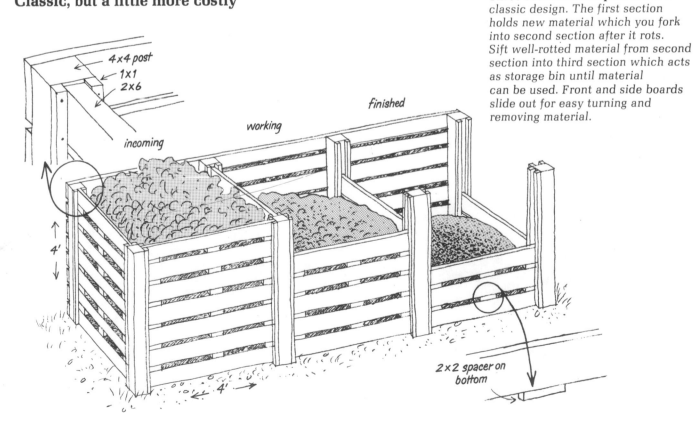

4x4 post
1x1
2x6

incoming
working
finished

4'
4'

2x2 spacer on bottom

What killed the petunias?

Sometimes a gardener runs into this special problem: certain plants do poorly regardless of care, or the whole garden grows too slowly, looks stunted, and has a high mortality rate. If this happens to you, examine the seven special soil problems and solutions listed below. If none of them provide an answer to your situation, turn to the section on bad drainage (page 14).

ALKALINE SOIL

Alkaline soil, common in light-rainfall areas of the Southwest, is soil that is high in calcium carbonate (lime) and certain other minerals. Many plants will grow well in a moderately alkaline soil, although camellias and other acid-loving plants will not.

Areas with softened water are quite likely to have alkaline soil. The sodium in soft water is good for household use but poor for plants. Hard water, on the other hand, is ideal for garden watering.

Large scale chemical treatment of extremely alkaline soils is expensive and complex. A better bet is to plant in raised beds and containers using a good soil mix.

ACID SOIL

Acid soil is at the other end of the scale from alkaline soil. It is most common in areas of heavy rainfall and is often associated with sandy soil (but ocean beaches are rarely or never acid).

Mildly acid soils cause little trouble, but an intense acid condition is highly undesirable for most plants.

Ground limestone will help to neutralize an acid-reacting soil, since all acid soils are low in calcium (lime). Your choice of fertilizers can be another very important factor in controlling acidity; some fertilizers can actually increase soil acidity.

Some plants—azaleas, rhododendrons, and camellias to name a few—prefer soil that is moderately acid.

SALTS IN THE SOIL

An excess of salt in the soil is a widespread problem in arid and semi-arid regions. It can prevent germination, or, if plants are already growing, it stunts them and in advanced cases burns the foliage and finally kills them. Its presence can usually be detected by a white deposit of salt on the surface of the soil. Salts in your water and fertilizer can remain in the soil. Periodic slow, deep watering will help wash the salts beyond plant roots.

NUTRIENT DEFICIENCY

Most soils, left to themselves, yield the three major plant nutrients—nitrogen, phosphorus, and potassium—only very slowly. Even the richest soil cannot continue to provide an ample amount of these vital elements year after year.

Fertilizers—either chemical or organic—are the quickest and easiest answer to a nutrient deficiency. Many balanced fertilizers containing all three major elements are available (see page 26). There are also formulations of nitrogen, phosphorus, or potassium compounds that provide these nutrients separately.

Manure and well rotted compost are also beneficial in varying degrees to nutrient-shy soils, but are more effective in their ability to build up the soil's humus supply.

CHLOROSIS—LACK OF IRON

If the leaves of some plants turn yellow, but veins stay green, it may be caused by an iron deficiency. Chelating (pronounced key-lating) agents or iron sulfate can help to control chlorosis. Buy either one at a nursery or garden store and follow label directions.

COMPACTED SOIL

When you build on filled land, the soil has been compacted purposely to certain standards. Also any trucks and bulldozers used in the construction of your home may have caused accidental packing of soil. Little will grow in compacted soil. To counteract the effect, grow a crop of deep-rooted grass such as annual rye, then plow it under before adding amendments. If you're planting trees, have a well digger dig some 3-foot-deep holes, then improve the removed soil with amendments and refill around the root ball.

SHALLOW SOIL

If there is a layer of hardpan within the top 18 inches, plant roots won't grow and water won't penetrate. There are two possible solutions: either drill through shallow hardpan to make a vertical gravel drain, or get advice from an engineer on how to install drain tile horizontally (see page 14).

Break through hardpan, fill well with peat moss and sand...

...or slope drain tile away from planting hole

drain tile

Tar paper on joint

fine gravel

thick hardpan

Working the soil

The best landscape plan in the world will turn into an empty dream if the plants grow poorly. So before you turn the first spadeful of earth, ponder this question: How has the weather been? If the dirt is gummy wet, wait until it dries out enough to crumble when you try to squeeze it into a handful. If it's brick hard, water deeply and then wait until it dries to the moist but crumbly stage. If your spade slides in easily, read on.

For deep cultivation, use double-digging

Dig trench *about 12 to 18 inches wide and 8 to 9 inches deep.*

Mix compost *or other soil amendments into the next level of soil.*

Move over *12 inches, mix soil, amendment; fill first trench.*

Work amendment *into bottom of new trench as you did before.*

Continue digging *and mixing until the entire area is completed.*

Mix soil *from first hole with amendment and fill remaining hole.*

Another way to double-dig

Remove spade's depth *of soil, putting it around sides of hole. Spade amendment into bottom soil. Mix amendment into removed soil layer, then refill the hole.*

SPADE OR SHOVEL?

The hard work of turning up the soil will seem a little easier if you use a **spade.** It should be square, sharp, and straight or nearly straight in its shank. When you push it into firm earth with your foot, you want all the force to go straight down the blade. And if you use a file to keep it sharpened, roots and clods of soil won't be major obstacles. A scoop-shaped **shovel,** with its pointed blade, should be used for mixing or turning loose materials. You handle it as if it were a combination of a spade and scoop. The point on the shovel helps you to slide it into the material and the concave blade keeps the material from sliding off as you lift and turn. A shovel blade is set at an angle to the shaft so it stays flat when you push it horizontally into a pile of material.

Dig with spade, scoop with shovel

In spading up small areas of soil, many gardeners make the mistake of turning each spadeful of earth completely over. If you make the same mistake, any weeds, leaves, or other debris in the soil will form a one-spade-deep barrier that cuts off air and water. Instead, you should lay the dirt on its side (against the previous shovelful) so the original surface is vertical to the ground (see sketch below).

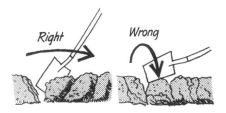

Right   *Wrong*

MACHINE POWER

Using a spade to turn the earth is fine for small areas, but for really big jobs you may want to rent or buy a power tiller. The three photographs below show the basic steps in power tilling, but you might consider another approach as well. Because a tiller is adjustable, it can either scratch the surface or dig down several inches. If you want to add amendments to packed soil but find it hard to make the tiller dig deep enough, start tilling at a shallow depth. Go over the area a second time (or even a third) with the tiller at a deeper setting each time. (Generally, the more powerful the tiller and the higher its horsepower, the deeper it can dig into the soil.)

In adding amendment, you should mix in a quantity that is from a quarter to a half of the finished volume of soil. (For more information on soil amendments, see pages 4—7.) Don't pile up so much amendment that the tiller can't penetrate the soil. To avoid this, start by adding the amendment in 2 or 3-inch layers, tilling in each layer. If the amendment you choose needs nitrogen, add part of the amount with each amendment layer. Finally, don't till in the same direction each time you add a layer of amendment. For the best mix the furrows should be at right angles to the furrows you made on your previous run.

Spread a 2 to 4-inch layer of soil amendment over soil with a rake; add nitrogen fertilizer if needed (see chart, page 6). Don't till yet.

Scatter superphosphate or bone meal (following package directions) for good root growth. If amendment is sawdust, also add iron chelate.

Cultivate in one direction, then at right angles, tilling the top 8 or 9 inches of soil. Repeat several times to mix soil evenly with amendment.

Putting prepared soil to work

Dig planting hole and pile removed soil beside it. Make pile of soil amendment half as big. Mix the two, add superphosphate, and mix again.

Place enough soil in hole to make top of root ball sit just above ground level. Adjust plant to best angle, then refill hole and form water basin.

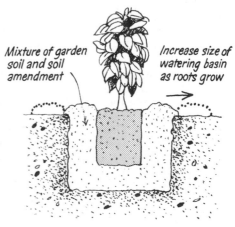

Mixture of garden soil and soil amendment

Increase size of watering basin as roots grow

Planting hole should look like this in cross section. Widen the water basin as plant grows so it is always wider than outer plant branches.

When water won't drain

You may find yourself digging a planting hole, filling it with water, then turning to the next job of adding amendments to the soil you've removed. An hour later you realize the hole is still full of water; even a day later the water's only down an inch.

Most plants won't live long in waterlogged soil. Even if they can stand the airless condition, they won't be able to tolerate the salts that build up from evaporation. What are your alternatives? You can build raised beds for your plants or simply use container plants (the only solution if your garden lies over solid rock). You may also be able to improve soil drainage if the problem is caused by a layer of hardpan or clay just below the surface, or if the soil is compacted.

TRY TO DIG TO A POROUS LAYER

Your soil may contain a shallow layer of hard or dense soil just under the surface, but the layers below may be porous. To test your soil consistency, use a posthole digger to dig down 2½ or 3 feet; check for a change in color and consistency. Also fill the hole with water to check drainage. If the water drains away in a relatively short time, this approach will work. (If you need to dig several holes, you may want to consider renting power equipment.)

Fill the hole a quarter of the depth with fine sand or sand and peat moss (this fine-grained material will help draw water downward). Set the plant in the hole so the joint between roots and trunk—called the "crown"—is higher than the surrounding soil. The crown is sensitive and should be in dry, airy soil, or even left uncovered.

Roughen up the sides of the planting hole so the roots can penetrate more easily as they grow. Add organic amendment to the soil you removed until a third to a half of the mix is amendment. If needed, add nitrogen (see directions in the soil amendment chart on pages 6 and 7), and blend in bone meal or superphosphate following package directions. And if your soil tends to be alkaline or you want to guard against chlorosis, add sulfur and iron chelate (see page 11).

If there isn't much topsoil over the hard under-layer, make oversized planting holes. Filled with improved soil, these holes act like giant containers. The roots will never be able to penetrate the surrounding unimproved soil, so the holes have to be big enough for the roots to mature and support the top growth. Here are suggested dimensions:

Large tree—6 feet wide by 3 feet deep
Small tree—5 feet wide by 3 feet deep
Large shrub—4 feet wide by 3 feet deep
Small shrub—2 feet wide by 2 feet deep
Flowers—plant in 18-inch-depth of improved soil

WHEN YOU CAN'T BREAK THROUGH

You may find the impermeable layer of soil just under the surface too thick to penetrate. The solution to this problem is to install a drainage system.

If the planting site is on high ground, dig a sloping ditch toward a driveway, street, or downslope. Place terra cotta or composition drain tiles into the planting hole, covering the joints with tar paper. Cover the entire drain with crushed rock and then with part of the amended soil you'll use to fill the planting hole.

If the ground is level, digging a sump hole is the only solution for getting water to drain. Dig a hole 3 to 4 feet wide and 4 to 5 feet deep right at the planting site or about a foot to one side. Add a 1-foot layer of fine sand and cover with fiberglass. If the sump hole is to one side, lay a piece of drain pipe from the planting hole to the sump, inclining it sharply downward from the planting hole into the sand. Then refill the sump hole. A sump hole usually is not a permanent solution, since silt will eventually fill it and make it useless; however, there is the chance that the plant roots may have broken their way into the hardpan by then and improved drainage by themselves.

In impermeable soil, you must set the plants a little above ground level to keep the crown in dry, airy soil. To keep above-surface soil in place, circle the plant with a low edging board.

MAJOR SURGERY FOR COMPACTED SOIL

Solid layers of soil that were compacted by bulldozers can be improved if you can put off your landscaping plans for a while and enlist the help of a landscape contractor who has heavy duty equipment. The soil must be cultivated to a depth of 18 inches or deeper. You then plant annual rye grass. The root system of rye grass is deep and wide and will break up compacted soil at a deeper level than you could reach with plowing. Keep the grass growing for 6 months to a year with regular watering. During this time, cut the grass once or twice, leaving the cuttings where they fall. Clipping the grass keeps it from going to seed and dying too soon.

When the grass is 6 to 10 months old, the landscape architect will have his men plow in the grass to a depth of 9 to 12 inches and add an organic amendment and any necessary nitrogen. You can then dig planting holes and set in your plants. Where possible, leave half the root ball above the natural surface and mound good soil around it. Cover the area around the plant with a two-inch layer of organic material. It will hold in moisture and you'll have to water less frequently (see the section on mulches, page 24). Once a year, spade the mulch into the soil and replace it with a new layer.

PLANTS FOR SOGGY SOIL

Some plants withstand the wet soil caused by bad drainage better than others. On the opposite page you'll find a listing of the plants that do the best job of tolerating wetness.

TREES

Quince (*Cydonia oblonga*). Deciduous tree with 2-inch flowers, edible fruit.

Red maple (*Acer rubrum*). Deciduous. For cool or coastal areas.

Sweet gum (*Liquidambar styraciflua*). Fall color, interesting seed pods.

Sycamore (*Platanus*). Messy fluff from seeds. Deciduous.

White alder (*Alnus rhombifolia*). Deciduous western native that may reach 90 feet.

Willow (*Salix*). Cuttings root quickly. Many shapes and sizes from weeping to shrubby.

SHRUBS

Oleander (*Nerium oleander*). Best in warm climates. Flower colors pink, white, yellow.

Pampas grass (*Cortaderia selloana*). Big grassy clumps produce feathery white plumes.

Privet (*Ligustrum*). Classic hedge plant, but can be small tree. Most are deciduous, some are evergreen.

BULBS

Iris. Beardless and Louisiana iris have flowers in white, yellow, pink, red, purple, many blues. Japanese iris blooms in July. Siberian iris has butterfly flowers on 2 to 3-foot stems.

ANNUALS

Calendula. Winter-blooming in mild areas. Flowers in orange and yellow.

Monkey flower (*Mimulus tigrinus*). Sprawling growth to 1 foot. Blooms spring and summer.

VINES

Cup-of-gold vine (*Solandra guttata*). Salt-tolerant evergreen with big, trumpet-shaped yellow flowers.

Hall's Japanese honeysuckle (*Lonicera japonica* 'Halliana'). Evergreen in warm climates. Strong perfume.

What's beneath the surface?

The soil sampling tube shown at right helps to keep a gardener informed about the condition of the normally invisible layer of soil in which his plants are rooting most actively.

Perhaps the most important function of the tube is testing for water penetration. The day after watering, take a core sample of the soil. It should be dark colored, and it should feel moist. If the soil is dry below the first 3 inches, you need to water for longer periods of time. If it's soggy near the top, then hard, then dry, the soil needs to be aerated. If you find a hard layer just below the surface, then your soil should be improved with amendments (see pages 4—7).

Another function of the soil sampling tube is to help you check for an even mix of amendments when you condition your soil. Blobs of pure clay or pure amendment mean that a more thorough mixing is needed. You can also check for root penetration and density by carefully crumbling a core sample to see how many root fibers appear at different levels. And still another function of the tube is to check for underground pests like root aphids or nematode worms.

Some gardeners use the soil sampling tube in feeding trees and big shrubs. Punch holes around the drip line and fill with dry or liquid fertilizer.

You can't find a soil tube just anywhere. Stores that stock scientific equipment sometimes have them, or can order one for you. If you still can't find one, call your county agricultural agent or a university department of agriculture to ask if they know of a mail order source.

Sample soil core *from lawn shows top two-thirds of sample is moist, the rest is dry. Lawn needs longer waterings for deeper penetration. Tube has marked scale.*

WATER
...making every drop count

Most garden plants get their moisture from the soil layers near the surface. Only a few plants—mainly grasses and trees—have roots that can reach down into the deeper layers. But the surface layers of soil are constantly losing water. The plants take it up through their roots and release it through their leaves during the day, particularly in hot weather. Also, as the sun heats the ground, moisture evaporates. Dry winds also cause evaporation. These sources of water loss are at their worst in hot climates with long, dry seasons and where water is scarce and expensive.

Below and on the following pages are suggestions and techniques for keeping the soil moist. By following these points you'll keep watering to a minimum and the watering you do will reach the plant roots instead of evaporating.

SOIL TYPE IS IMPORTANT

When you wet soil, the water penetrates according to the soil type and structure (for descriptions of soil types see page 4).

Each soil type has a holding capacity. It will retain a certain amount of water and allow the rest to sink deeper. For example, dense clay soil holds more water than porous sand. Until the holding capacity of a layer of soil is exceeded, no water will sink to the next layer. Because of this, any watering you do may only penetrate the first 2 or 3 inches, leaving the soil beneath dry. In addition, dense soil won't accept water as quickly as porous soil. Heavy watering may only create rivers that flow into the gutter and leave much of the soil dry.

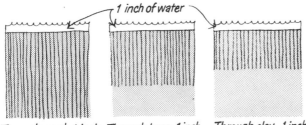

Through sand, 1 inch of water penetrates 12 inches   Through loam, 1 inch of water penetrates 6–10 inches   Through clay, 1 inch of water penetrates 4–5 inches

Differences in soil structure also affect water penetration. If you lay topsoil on a different kind of native soil, the water is likely to go as far as the boundary line between the types and then just sit or flow away to the side. The same thing happens when you place a nursery plant in a hole and put your garden soil back in the hole around the root ball. Water outside the root ball won't go in, and water inside won't go out. And since roots only go where there's moisture, they may never grow out of the original nursery soil.

For all these reasons, you should amend the soil as described on pages 4–7. Amendments help to lighten dense soil, hold water in porous soil, and create a transitional zone between the soil types.

DEEP SOAKING FOR PROPER ROOT GROWTH

If you water for a brief period each day, you will only wet the upper few inches of soil. This happens because you haven't watered enough to exceed the holding capacity of that layer of soil and force water down. The roots of your plants will stay in the moist upper layer. Because moisture evaporates quickly, you'll waste time and water using this method. And, if you forget to water or there's a hot spell in July, you may lose a lot of plants. Another drawback of frequent watering is that it encourages growth of weed seeds, fungus, and disease organisms.

Light watering makes shallow roots. Hot spell may damage plant

Deep watering sends roots down to cool soil

The best general watering plan is to soak the soil deeply and not water again until the top few inches of soil begin to dry out. Plant roots will extend into deeper soil where they stay cool, and any weeds at the top won't have a chance to grow. If you have dense soil, water slowly so the water has time to penetrate. It may take hours for water to reach the 12 to 18-inch level. To be sure it has, wait a day or two, then dig up a spadeful or take a core sample using a special tool (see page 15).

WIND CAN STEAL WATER

When you turn on a sprinkler on a windy day, a good amount of the water may be carried away before it can penetrate the soil. Some is carried away as windborne particles; some evaporates from the surface before it sinks in. If possible, turn on sprinklers only in still weather. If it's necessary to water on a windy day, use a soaker.

Wind also steals water that the plants draw up and release through their leaves. In still weather, the air around the leaf surface is humid, so the loss of moisture is not as great. Windy weather causes a more rapid water loss from leaves and may dry up plants so much

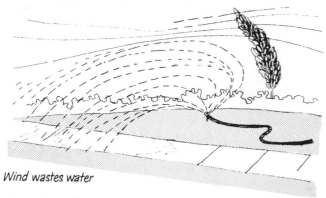

Wind wastes water

that they burn or die. If your property sits in the path of a prevailing wind, arrange your garden in such a way that plants will have a windbreak. Trees and tall plants placed on the windy side will help; but solid fences or masonry walls may not. Because wind flows like water, it will come over the top of a solid barrier in a wave, crashing down on the other side. If the windbreak lets some of the wind through, it creates turbulence on the lee side, breaking up the wave into eddies that do less damage.

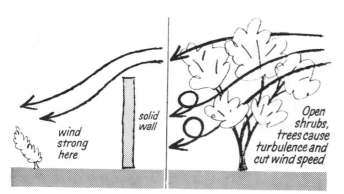

wind strong here / solid wall / Open shrubs, trees cause turbulence and cut wind speed

UNDERSTANDING THE DRIP LINE

Plant roots usually spread as wide as the plant foliage. In taking up water and nutrients, the tips of the root mass play the most active part. The term "drip line" simply means the circle beneath the outer leaves of a plant where most rainwater drips to the ground. The effect is similar to water dripping off an umbrella.

If you build a low, circular dike of earth just outside the drip line of a plant, you have a watering basin. Put your soaker in it and let the water penetrate. The roots have time to absorb it because the branches shade the area, cutting down evaporation. You can use the same watering basin to feed the plant.

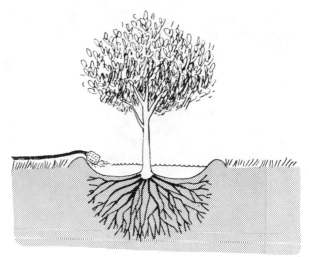

KEEPING POTS MOIST

Keeping container plants moist is often difficult because there is only a limited amount of soil to hold moisture. Also, water can evaporate through the sides and bottom of many containers. In warm weather, some container plants may need water several times a day. Here are some solutions to this problem:

• Repot plants regularly. Pot bound plants have no reserve of moist soil outside the root area.

• Soak the soil. Submerge small pots in a tub of water until air bubbles stop. Run water into larger pots until it flows freely from the drainage holes.

• Use double pots. Put small pots in larger ones and insulate the space between with gravel or moist peat moss.

• Group pots together. Five or six pots placed together help to protect each other from heat.

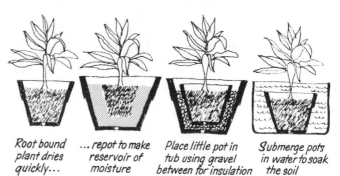

Root bound plant dries quickly... / ...repot to make reservoir of moisture / Place little pot in tub using gravel between for insulation / Submerge pots in water to soak the soil

What size garden hose?

Garden hoses, as you can see by the photographs below, come in different sizes—and in this instance, we mean **diameter,** an important consideration that many gardeners fail to understand until after they've made their purchase. Regardless of what your water pressure happens to be, the output you get from it through a hose is in direct ratio to the hose's inside diameter.

The smallest diameter commonly sold—7/16 inch—is too small to be recommended for general gardening use, so it isn't considered here. Standard sizes are ½, ⅝, and ¾-inch diameter. A hose of 1-inch diameter is manufactured, but it's difficult to use and is seldom available to home gardeners.

When you buy a hose, avoid the super-bargains—they seldom last very long and can cause you much trouble and lost time. The best indication of a good hose is a guarantee. Don't buy one that isn't guaranteed or warranted. It's that simple.

A ½-inch hose filled this 5-gallon jar approximately ⅓ full in 15 seconds. If you have big, thirsty trees and shrubs to water, buy a larger size.

A ⅝-inch hose delivered twice the amount of water as the size at left, in same period of time. This size is practical for almost any home garden.

Big ¾-inch hose filled jar in 15-seconds. With pressure of 50 pounds per square inch, it put an inch of water on 1,500-sq. ft. lawn in 39 minutes.

Light weight and easy storage are the advantage of a ½-inch hose. Fifty feet weighs only 6 pounds. Especially good for container watering.

Slightly heavier, 50 feet of ⅝-inch hose weighs only 1½ pounds more than size at left. Good buy where lots are large, or where water pressure is low.

Very heavy ¾-inch size weighs 11 pounds for 50 feet and is hard to store. It's long wearing, and is a necessity with some kinds of sprinklers.

Sprinkler patterns

Choosing a sprinkler can be a dilemma to the home gardener, what with the ever-increasing variety of kinds to select from.

Generally, however, different sprinklers can be grouped according to the kind of watering pattern they make. A study of the five patterns shown here should help you to decide which sprinkler might be the best one for you.

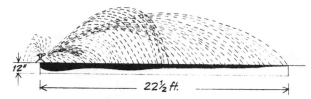

Pattern #1 *is effective if you move sprinkler to obtain overlap. Oscillating type makes this pattern, as does the rotating "machine gun" type, which shoots rapid-fire jets.*

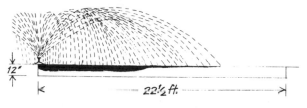

Pattern #2. *Most water drops on inside; you must make successive overlaps. Several sprinklers work this way, including "fixed head" and whirling baffle types.*

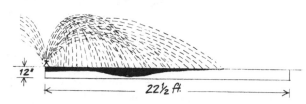

Pattern #3. *Useful but erratic; most water falls from 4 to 8 feet out. Some examples: plastic tube soakers; types with revolving arms; those which squirt from sieve holes.*

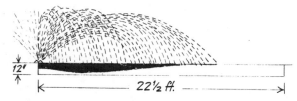

Pattern #4. *Cone spray soaks only a small area; for best results, turn water to half-pressure, move sprinkler often. One cone spray has two big holes like owl's eyes.*

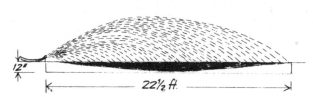

Pattern #5. *Fan spray throws most water 7 to 14 feet from sprinkler head. Example: nailhead spike type, which sprays water through a slit in its head.*

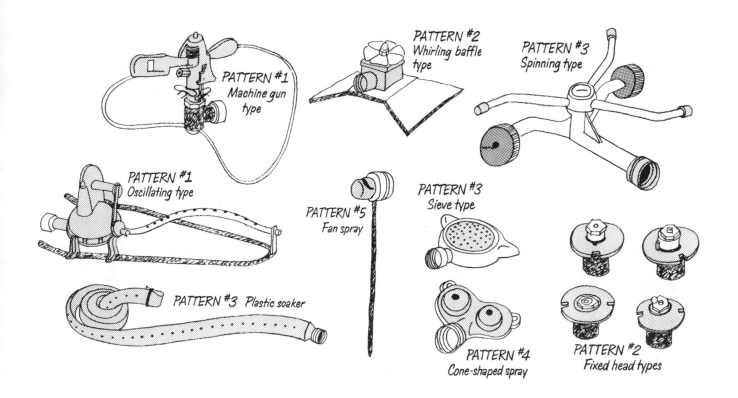

PATTERN #1 Machine gun type

PATTERN #2 Whirling baffle type

PATTERN #3 Spinning type

PATTERN #1 Oscillating type

PATTERN #5 Fan spray

PATTERN #3 Sieve type

PATTERN #3 Plastic soaker

PATTERN #4 Cone-shaped spray

PATTERN #2 Fixed head types

Hose accessories

Almost everyone needs a hose for the garden even in an area that receives a lot of rain. Illustrated on these two pages are some parts and accessories for repairing, using, and storing hoses. You'll also find information on the various drip watering installations that are useful in watering certain kinds of plants.

When you buy hose repair parts, be sure you have the right kind. For example, connectors or hose ends with a circle of teeth that bite into the outside of the hose are for rubber hoses, whereas the kind with a screw-in core are for plastic hoses. If you can, take your hose with you to make sure the repair part fits.

HOSE CONNECTORS AND REPAIR PARTS

FOR RUBBER HOSE ONLY

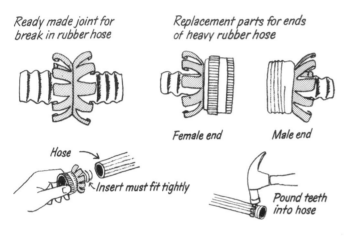

Ready made joint for break in rubber hose

Replacement parts for ends of heavy rubber hose

Female end

Male end

Hose

Insert must fit tightly

Pound teeth into hose

FOR PLASTIC HOSE ONLY

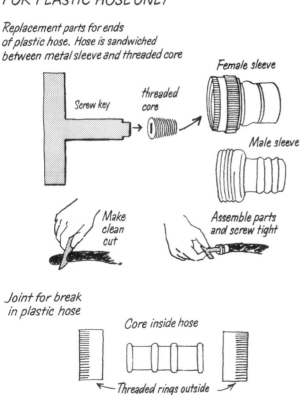

Replacement parts for ends of plastic hose. Hose is sandwiched between metal sleeve and threaded core

Screw key

threaded core

Female sleeve

Male sleeve

Make clean cut

Assemble parts and screw tight

Joint for break in plastic hose

Core inside hose

Threaded rings outside

HAND NOZZLES

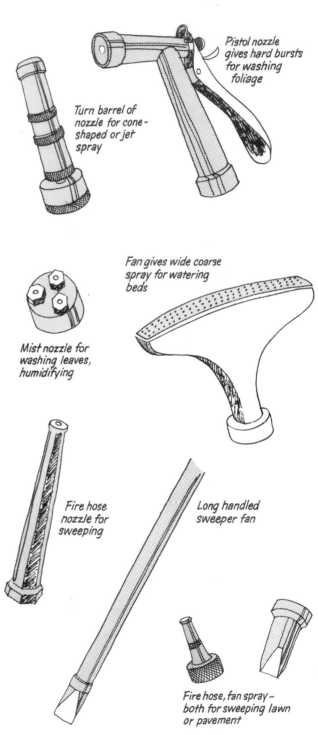

Pistol nozzle gives hard bursts for washing foliage

Turn barrel of nozzle for cone-shaped or jet spray

Mist nozzle for washing leaves, humidifying

Fan gives wide coarse spray for watering beds

Fire hose nozzle for sweeping

Long handled sweeper fan

Fire hose, fan spray—both for sweeping lawn or pavement

SEVEN SOAKERS

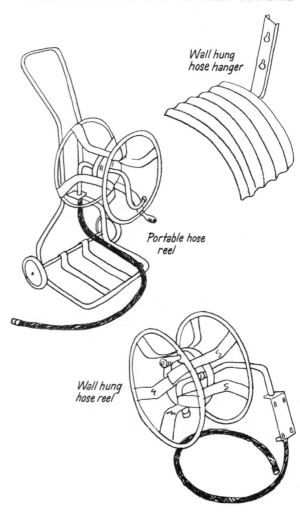

Extender tube for many soaker heads. Use it to reach up or across a wide bed

Heads for coarse high volume spray

Flow heads for large volume of water without gouging soil

These two flow heads come with extenders

Soaker hose comes in plastic or canvas. Place holes down for soak, up for fine spray

THREE WAYS TO STORE HOSES

Wall hung hose hanger

Portable hose reel

Wall hung hose reel

Drip irrigation

The easiest and most efficient way to water plants that were set out in a regular pattern is to use one of the systems shown at right.

For hedges, ground cover plants, and rows of vegetables, you can buy a collection of spikelike inserts that pierce a hose and let water out. The inserts are of varied kinds that let the water drip, bubble, or squirt out. You first arrange the hose so it runs by the plants (use stakes to keep it in place), then push the inserts into the hose wherever you want water. This watering system is made by several manufacturers and marketed under different names, but if you describe what you want at a garden supply house, you should find it.

The second type of watering system (called "spaghetti hose") consists of a length of rigid or flexible plastic pipe and thin plastic tubes (the tubes can be cut to any convenient length). You drill holes in the pipe where you need them and cement a length of tubing in each hole. A lead weight attached to the tubes keeps them in place in a pot. This system is especially useful for watering large numbers of containers or even house plants. If you have trouble finding the parts, ask your nurseryman if he can order them for you.

Spikes in hose are good for watering individual plants.

Thin tubes drip water from pipe into separate containers.

Watering vegetables

A vegetable patch often ends up in a far corner of the garden where it's difficult to water. For example, the circular vegetable and herb garden illustrated below was laid out on a large country lot far from a hose bib.

The owner had no place for planting vegetable beds near the house, so the remote corner seemed to be the only answer. If you have a similar problem, you'll quickly notice how tiresome it becomes to connect several hoses together, carry them from place to place, and then run back to change the sprinkler several times. You can avoid these complications by planting a circular garden like the one illustrated below and placing a circular head sprinkler on a stand in the center. (Whenever you sprinkle vegetables from overhead, let the water run long enough so it can soak in deeply, then allow the upper soil layer to dry out before watering again.)

Remember that the layout of a vegetable garden requires careful planning to assure that every plant receives the amount of water it needs for healthy rapid growth. For example, in a circular garden, tall plants should be on the outside of the circle with low plants in the center.

Circular garden *gets its water from a machine-gun sprinkler on stand at center. Diagram of garden is at left below.*

For vegetables that require deep root watering but dislike dampening of foliage, consider one of the two watering methods illustrated at right. The first method is for vining plants that produce fruit that lies on the ground (pumpkins and squash, for example). Plant your seed in a central hollow and train the vines to grow away from it. You can then soak the root area without wetting the foliage and fruit.

An alternative to the method above is to plant in long, low mounds of soil and dig watering trenches in between each mound. You'll need a soaker for this method to make sure that water flows the length of the trench (for types of soakers available, see page 21).

The second method for watering vegetables is a variation of the trench irrigation method. You plant small crops of plants, like lettuces or cabbage, along both sides of the trench. Soil just under their leaves stays dry.

For those who choose to dig irrigation trenches, remember that if you aim a trench downhill (even if the slope is gradual), you'll waste water and may wash away soil and plants. So take this precaution: First check the evenness of the ground with a carpenter's level. Then stretch a string to serve as a digging guide.

Pumpkins, squash *watered at center; plants grow outward.*

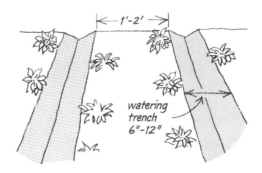

Place plants *in rows alongside irrigating trenches.*

Watering containers

The watering of container plants may seem almost too simple to mention. However, if you've ever nursed a dozen or so plants through a hot summer, you know it's not so easy. (For more container gardening information, see page 64.)

There is no foolproof watering formula. It depends on such variables as soil mix, type of container, location of the plant in the garden, and climate. Keep in mind that the soil in most containers dries out much faster than in a garden bed. If you're new to container gardening, you may want to check the soil moisture of your plants every day or so; you'll quickly learn which plants need more water and which ones need less. Here are some methods for doing your watering efficiently (for other suggestions on keeping container plants moist, see page 17):

Special watering situations may require special tools; large hardware stores and nurseries stock watering accessories. An on-off valve may help conserve water, but be sure your hose is solid.

Don't squirt the top. It acts like an umbrella, wastes water

Rinsing off foliage is not a good watering practice; little water reaches the roots as foliage deflects it. Water the soil first, then spray foliage to remove dust and pests.

A pot liner or drip tray protects the surface under the pot from stains. Put a layer of pebbles or gravel in the tray so pot sits above any water that drains through; water will evaporate and raise humidity.

Cork drain hole of hanging pot before watering, then leave it in place for 10 minutes to soak the soil more thoroughly.

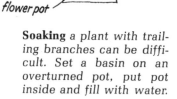

Soaking a plant with trailing branches can be difficult. Set a basin on an overturned pot, put pot inside and fill with water.

Don't use a strong jet of water from a hose; it may gouge out a hole in the soil and expose plant roots. A soaker head, with or without a long handle, is best for container watering; or use a hose with less and slower water flow.

Dry root ball may shrink away from container sides. Water runs around the outside without soaking the soil. If there is space between soil and pot, scrape soil from root ball to fill gap or add extra soil mix. Water until soil is soaked.

Mulch saves water and weeding

A mulch is simply a covering for the soil. Gardeners have used almost any material as a mulch, including old newspaper, foot-deep straw, grass clippings, tree leaves, roofing paper, and plastic. These and many other materials will work if they satisfy these two basic conditions: The mulch should help to retain water in the soil on hot days, and it should smother weeds. A third but less important condition is that it looks attractive. (Mulch can also insulate plants in cold weather.)

If you leave soil uncovered, hot sun and wind will quickly dry it out, forcing you to water more often. The additional water may also produce unwanted weeds. Another disadvantage of bare soil is that the top layer often gets too hot for good root growth. Even if you manage to keep the soil moist, your plants won't grow as well as they should.

Mulching accomplishes a number of things that are illustrated below.

Even though sun will heat the surface of a mulch, the soil below is insulated because the mulch holds air. And any moisture in the soil has a hard time evaporating through the differently textured mulch. Because the soil is kept cool, the roots stay near the surface, ready to take fertilizer. Most weeds are smothered, but those that grow are rooted in the loose mulch and come up easily. You should not let mulches build up against the trunk or stem of a plant (commonly called the "crown") because the trunk may rot if it stays moist too long.

You can use any of the materials mentioned here as mulch, but also check the other materials listed in the soil amendment chart, pages 6 and 7. (Some of these materials should be used along with a nitrogen fertilizer as indicated in the chart.) When you choose a mulch, consider the following:

● It should be fairly easy to wet. For example, peat moss dries out quickly, and once dry it may become impermeable.

● It should be dense enough not to blow away.

Fir bark is a good choice for a mulch, since it meets all of the above requirements even when finely ground (for certain very windy areas, you may wish to use large chips).

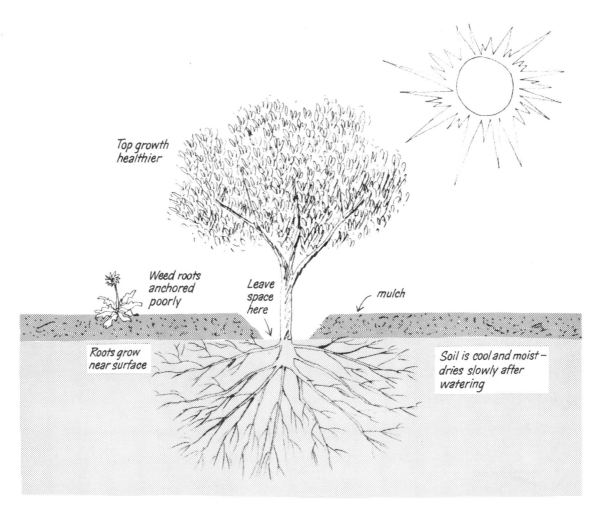

Top growth healthier

Weed roots anchored poorly

Leave space here

mulch

Roots grow near surface

Soil is cool and moist — dries slowly after watering

Three inches of mulch keeps the root zone of a plant cool and moist even in hot weather. Mulched plants may grow twice as big as those without a mulch, produce better flowers and fruit. Plant roots grow thicker, and water won't evaporate as rapidly. Weeds may grow on mulch surface, are easy to pull out.

Powdery mulch may blow away in wind

Dense fir bark mulch stays in place

Most organic mulches should be dug into the soil every year or two and a new layer added. Spade the mulch under as winter begins and replace it just before weed growth starts in spring. Where winters are mild and rainy, you may want to replace the mulch immediately to maintain weed control.

Turn mulch into soil in fall, add new layer right away, or wait until spring

Dig no more than 3" to 4" deep inside drip line

To measure the effect of mulching, scientists in Connecticut used four different cheap mulching materials around petunias. They used old grocery bags, double layers of newspaper, roofing paper, and 3 inches of grass clippings. The mulched plants grew better than those in bare earth, but those with a grass clippings mulch grew twice as big. There were also more flowers on the mulched plants. Surprisingly, nematode worms (a common pest in some soils) were less numerous under all the mulches except the roofing paper.

One disadvantage of a grass mulch is that it tends to rot and breed flies. A 2 or 3-inch bark mulch is a good substitute for grass.

Mulches can also be used around trees, in play areas, or in other areas where you don't want to plant grass or ground cover but don't want to pave either. You can use rock, gravel, or the largest size of bark chips. Because these mulches do not shut out light, weeds may be a problem. You can solve it by covering the ground with black polyethylene plastic before spreading the mulch.

The same black plastic is also valuable in the vegetable garden. It tends to absorb extra heat and warm the soil, so root growth is fast at the beginning of the season

and the amount of the crop is greater at the end. Before spreading the plastic, prepare the soil by adding a complete fertilizer and watering thoroughly. Leave enough room between the sheets of plastic for planting rows of small seeds (carrots, lettuce, or radishes). For larger seeds (beans, peas, or squash) make planting holes in the plastic. The gaps and holes will let water through, and because moisture evaporation is cut down by the overall covering, you won't have to water as much.

River rocks resembling the bottom of a stream bed act as a decorative mulch over tree roots, keep weeds down.

Rocks, pebbles arranged in geometric shapes serve as mulch under pine tree. Falling pine needles add to mulch.

FERTILIZERS
...and how to use them

This may surprise you, but green plants manufacture their own food. From the atmosphere they take in water, sunlight, and carbon dioxide to create sugar and starch. From the soil they extract water and nitrogen compounds which they use to make protein for forming tissues and seeds. Plants also take small amounts of other elements from the soil to grow properly. Besides nitrogen, the two most important elements any plant needs are phosphorus and potassium. Phosphorus helps plants to form genetic material. Potassium aids in cell division and in manufacturing food.

Soils containing a lot of organic material provide a healthy environment for the fungus and bacteria which transform nitrogen and other elements into usable compounds the plants can absorb. Fungus and bacteria are also needed to break down the organic material.

If a plant can do this much on its own, then why should you ever need to use a fertilizer or amend the soil? The answer is simple: In nature, whatever comes from the soil usually returns to it. But a gardener normally carries away many nutrients in the form of fruit, flowers, and spent plants. By fertilizing your plants, you make sure they'll always have the various elements they need. By adding organic material to the soil, you provide a healthy environment for the growth of soil organisms which help to keep the natural food-producing cycle going.

BUYING CHEMICAL FERTILIZER

Many different fertilizers are available in dry, liquid, and tablet form. Those containing all the needed food elements are called complete fertilizers. Others contain a high percentage of only one element such as nitrogen, phosphorus, or potassium. Before you buy a fertilizer check to see how much of these main elements it contains. Somewhere on the package you'll find three numbers, such as 10-8-6. The first number refers to the percentage of nitrogen, the second phosphorus, and the last potassium. If one of the numbers is zero, then that particular element is not included in the mixture.

You may find that your plants don't always require all three elements. For example, if you see planting instructions that recommend mixing superphosphate or bone meal (an organic fertilizer high in phosphorus) into the planting soil, you are adding phosphorus for strong root growth. Other elements may not be needed at the time of planting.

BUYING ORGANIC FERTILIZER

You'll find that organic fertilizers are made of varied materials such as cotton seed meal, blood meal, bone meal, activated sewage sludge, hoof-and-horn meal, or guano (bird or bat droppings). Listed on the package you'll find the percentage of each of the three main elements. Most organic fertilizers are rather slow in giving up their nutrients since bacterial action is required before nutrients can be released.

Some people think that manure and compost are fertilizers. Both may contain tiny amounts of usable nutrients (manure is typically about 1-1-1), but they are best used as soil amendments to improve texture and promote the growth of soil bacteria. The bacteria in turn help your plants to take nourishment from the soil.

USING FERTILIZERS

Labels on packaged fertilizer give instructions for their use. Look for the amounts suggested for an area of square feet, or for the amount to be mixed in a gallon of water.

Most plants should be fed in the spring when leaf growth begins and again about three months later. If winters are mild, you can also feed plants in early fall.

Some plants require special feeding schedules. Roses grow so rapidly that you can feed them the recommended dose every six weeks. Rhododendrons, azaleas, and camellias like nutrients as their blooms fade and again six weeks later. Fruit trees benefit from a feeding about three weeks before they bloom. Vegetables need some plant food when their seeds sprout, and again when the plants are established (leaf vegetables require a high-nitrogen food). Container plants and such fast-growing plants as fuchsias and begonias can use a very light feeding once a week. (A light feeding is about ¼ of what the label recommends.)

Fertilizer comes in dry or liquid form. To help a dry fertilizer be as effective as possible, you may want to dig it into the soil around the root zone. (A phosphoric acid fertilizer, such as superphosphate or bone meal, is normally applied in this way.) For established plants, work the fertilizer into the upper soil layer, being careful not to damage plant roots. For rows of young seedlings, dig a shallow trench on each side of the plants about four inches away and put in the proper amount of fertilizer. Whether you use the liquid or dry form, the fertilizer must be watered into the soil thoroughly or it will do no good.

Feeding trees and large shrubs

Trees and large shrubs can be fed as soon as the soil warms up in the spring. You can use any of the three feeding methods listed below. Be sure to place the fertilizer in the feeder root area, and to keep the trees and shrubs well watered throughout the growing season.

Root plug feeding. This method works best in areas with moderate rainfall and mild climate. Fertilizer used this way must have sufficient water to make it available to nearby roots, yet not so much as to leach it out of the root zone.

Use an auger (you can buy one at a garden supply store) to drill holes in a circle just inside the drip line. Make holes 18 to 24 inches apart (the sandier the soil, the closer the holes, since follow-up watering in sandy soil will distribute nutrients downward quite rapidly but laterally not very far). Don't drill down too far—just to the surface root zone.

Use a complete fertilizer, carefully following package directions as to the amount to be used and dividing by the number of holes you are going to fill. Before inserting the fertilizer in the holes, mix it with an equal amount of sand. Irrigate immediately and thoroughly; otherwise you'll burn the roots.

Liquid feeding. This is particularly good in dry soil regions because the nutrients are in a form immediately available to the tree. A follow-up application in 2 months is advisable.

Check for feeder roots *at the drip line by slicing out a piece of soil with a sharp spade and crumbling it. If you find a network of fine roots, apply fertilizer at this point. If not, keep searching toward the tree trunk.*

Home gardeners can use a hollow tube into which are inserted soluble fertilizer pellets, or venturi tube attachments for liquid concentrates; both devices attach to the garden hose. Insert the tube into the soil to a depth of

about 2 feet; water pressure forces the solution out to the roots. Holes should be about 18 inches apart, just inside the drip line.

Surface feeding. This method is popular in heavy rainfall areas. You can apply fertilizer by surface spreading or by digging small depressions at regular intervals and

filling with either liquid or dry fertilizer. However, you must water thoroughly when you apply either type (200 gallons of water is not too much). Remember, too, that surface plants under a tree will absorb some of the nutrient before it can reach the tree-root level.

One-sided watering *causes an uneven root system, with most of the growth on the watered side. Try to water evenly to stimulate new root growth all around the tree before applying one of the many fertilizers available.*

PEST CONTROL
...the common sense way

Many people who began gardening between 1940 and 1970 believed spraying everything in the garden with poisons was the only way to cope with plant pests and disease.

Since then, many gardeners have found that this cure can be worse than the problem. Pests and plant diseases are primarily a nuisance where one crop is planted in a large area. A pest that attacks only wheat or peaches would find a paradise in a field of wheat or a grove of peaches. Massive destruction by insects, mites, or diseases seldom happens in a garden with a wide variety of plants.

PREVENTIVE GARDEN MAINTENANCE

You can keep your garden relatively healthy without using chemical sprays by taking these two preliminary measures: Keep the soil in good shape by adding soil amendments and nutrients (see pages 6–7 and page 26) and remove any plant that is badly damaged by pests, or that is wilted or moldy. If you want to replace a damaged plant with a similar kind, ask your nurseryman about disease or pest-resistant varieties.

Once you have established a healthy garden, keep it clean. Rake up any debris such as fallen leaves and fruit (either compost, see page 10, or discard this debris; be careful not to compost diseased plant parts). Dig mulches into the ground each year, and replace them with fresh layers. Wash off foliage regularly (use a hose nozzle to direct the spray of water) to keep it free of dust and pests. Remove any spent flowers and foliage.

PICKING OFF PLANT EATERS

Whenever you're out in the garden, be sure to look for pests under a few leaves of each plant. If you squash or rub them off as soon as you notice them, you may not need a pesticide later on. And since many pests are sea-

sonal, they may disappear by themselves if you can keep them under control for the time being. If a hard squirt of water from a hose won't wash away a few aphids, rub them off by hand. You can squash caterpillars and beetles or you can put them in a paper bag and burn or discard it. To catch slugs and snails, place a few boards here and there, then turn them over every morning and remove the pests.

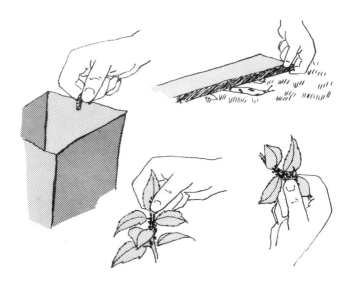

MANY CREATURES ARE HELPFUL

Some creatures do more good than harm. Avoid destroying those that eat other garden pests. Remember that a poison spray will kill the good bugs along with the bad ones. Turn to pages 34 and 35 for descriptions and photographs of some of the helpful insects and animals that you should encourage to stay in your garden. You'll learn to recognize ladybugs and their larvae, lacewings and their larvae, baby mantises (more numerous than adults), predatory wasps, insect-eating birds, and other tiny pest destroyers. Even though earwigs occasionally attack seedlings, flowers, or fruit, they will also eat regiments of aphids.

Before you aim a deadly spray at an infested plant, look around for helpful insects. If you see some, wait

insects as ants and earwigs. Most nurseries carry a sticky adhesive material that you paint around the base of the tree trunk. The pests will stick to the painted area on their way up the tree. You'll need to apply a new layer of material every few weeks because it gradually loses its stickiness as it collects dust or chaff. Check by touching it with your fingers whenever you pass by.

a few days before spraying to give them a chance to eat their fill of unwanted pests.

PROTECTION WITHOUT POISON

If you can't control garden pests by washing or rubbing them off, squashing them, or letting their natural enemies do the job, don't give up hope. There are alternatives which are deadly to pests yet harmless to other life. For sedentary bugs like aphids, make a strong solution of soap (not detergent) and water using 3 tablespoons of soap flakes in a gallon of tepid water. Using your tank or hose end sprayer, cover the infested plant with suds, wait a few hours, and then wash the plant off with plain water. Mineral oil sprays—sold in nurseries—do a similar job.

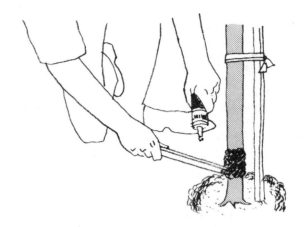

If plant seedlings are being chewed, try putting a jar or can over them at sundown and removing it in the morning. Push the jar into the soil a bit to prevent nocturnal chewers from getting under the rim. Don't forget to remove the covers in the morning or your seedlings will cook in the trapped heat under the cover.

Fruit trees are sometimes attacked by such climbing

SPRAY IF YOU MUST

Poisonous sprays are a touchy subject with some people, since the reports in books and newspapers about ecological damage or human illness that seems to be traceable to insecticide. However, most nurseries carry a number of spray materials which kill insects and disease organisms but are harmless to most other creatures. Some of these products contain sulfur or copper. Others, such as pyrethrum or rotenone, are made from the leaves and roots of certain plants. Limit your use of any of these sprays to afflicted plants only. The small portable pressurized tank sprayer is the easiest to use. It holds just enough mixture for small jobs, so you're never tempted to spray other plants with leftover spray.

(For more information on pest controls, turn to the chart on page 31.)

A final note: the loss of a few leaves or flowers does little real harm to a plant. Many lovely and productive gardens contain plants with chewed leaves and less than perfect flowers, but these imperfections are overlooked if the garden is healthy in all other respects.

Killing the killers

The chart on the opposite page suggests ways to control common garden pests. You'll find the non-toxic controls listed on the left side of the dark line. The chemical controls are listed on the right. Some of these chemicals are used as active ingredients in other chemical mixtures. These mixtures are scientifically tested for the compatibility of each ingredient. You should never try to mix different ingredients on your own.

Chemical controls should be handled and stored carefully. Before using one, read the instructions on the label. If you're spraying vegetables, the instructions will suggest how long to wait before harvest (guard against cutting these time periods short). When you're finished spraying, thoroughly wash your equipment, your hands and other exposed skin, and any clothing that came into direct contact with the spray. Then, for the safety of children and animals, store the chemical under lock and key. Make sure that any measuring spoons you use to measure quantity are stored the same way so they will not be used accidentally in the household.

To avoid mixing too much spray, use a 1-quart, graduated measuring cup rather than a 1-gallon measure so that you can easily calculate the amount you need. Remember that three teaspoons equal one tablespoon.

Tank sprayers are easier to handle (and less wasteful) than the extremely fast hose-end sprayers. If you intend to use any chemical that kills vegetation, such as weed oil, use a separate sprayer for it.

When you have finished spraying, be sure to wash and rinse sprayers and sprayer parts. Before you spray another time, rinse and wipe off all parts. A bit of chaff, a speck of dirt, or a little dried-up spray material can block tiny holes and give you hours of trouble and frustration.

Below are some suggestions for using the various controls listed in the chart headings.

Adhesive barriers. Check their stickiness frequently, since long exposure to the atmosphere can make them ineffective.

Hand methods. Gloves are recommended for those who dislike the feel of squashing unwanted pests. If you can't squash a bug even with gloves on, put your collection of pests in a paper bag and burn it. Another method is to put the pests in a jar and fill it with water; cap it overnight and dump it the next day.

Still another way to deal with pests is to place a few twists of newspaper in the garden in the evening; it will collect those countless earwigs who like to push into tiny spaces. This collection should be burned.

Because slugs and snails like dampness and protection from sun, a shingle or board placed in the garden will attract them. You then have the option of squashing them or putting them into a bag, adding salt, and discarding. Whichever method you choose, be sure to look out for their eggs which look like small clusters of pearls.

Certain underground pests such as cutworms and various grubs may suddenly appear when you work the soil, but it's easy to chop them up. Spadework, too, is sometimes an effective way to control ants. If you see an anthill, use a spade to turn over the soil, hoping that one spadeful will kill the queen. Without her, the workers will die.

To control flies, you can use the swatter—still a popular and effective tool. Sticky paper is another well-known method; it does a good job in sheds, lathhouses and other out-of-the-way corners. The paper comes in a roll inside a cardboard cylinder. Unroll it and pin it in a dark corner near the ceiling. Flies are attracted by its odor. Once the surface is well covered with dead flies, you throw the strip away and hang up a new one.

Dusting sulfur and lime sulfur. Before using these controls, carefully read the instructions on the label to make sure you are using them in the right season.

Water jet. Select a hose nozzle that adjusts for different sprays or a pistol type that delivers sudden, sharp blasts of water. Then look for your prey. Aphids are green or dark-colored and collect mainly on young growth and buds. Where they are very dense, put your hand behind the bud or branch as you hose them off; a little rubbing with your fingers will also help. Once on the ground, aphids rarely return to the plants.

Spittle bugs generally appear in spring and hide in little blobs of the foam they create. A direct hit from the water jet will knock them to the ground where they quickly die.

Spider mites are tiny red bugs that resemble spiders and live in a type of a web under leaves. If the underside of a leaf looks dusty or clouded, the mites may already be there. They love dust but hate dampness. Turn your hose nozzle up and spray upward from the base of the plant to clean the underside of the foliage.

If birch trees or other plants feel sticky, aphids are probably at work dripping honeydew. Wash the plant off thoroughly or a nasty black fungus will grow on it.

Metaldehyde. This chemical is a relative of wood alcohol (methanol). Slugs and snails love it for some reason, even though it's fatal. It comes in liquid or bait form. The bait consists of meal or pellets. Although some manufacturers add other poison to the bait, it's not necessary to make the chemical effective. Try to get metaldehyde mixed with bran; it is not harmful to birds and pets. Put the bait in a little dish under a garden shed or put it in a paper plate under a porch or deck. Snails or slugs often die on the spot. If so, just discard the plate or rinse it off over the trash pile or compost heap.

Other sprays. When you need a poisonous spray, use it carefully and make it count. Spray only those plants that are suffering from insect or mite damage. First rinse the plants off with water. Then spray the leaves, starting at the bottom of the plant and working upward. Finish by spraying the upper surfaces of the leaves.

Contact poisons. Pyrethrum, rotenone, ryania, sabadilla, and nicotine sulfate are all contact poisons—they must come into direct contact with the insect to kill it. These poisons are made from plant parts. Pyrethrum comes from a kind of chrysanthemum. Rotenone comes from the cube plant and is a ketone, like the flavor in whiskey. The nicotine in nicotine sulfate comes from tobacco.

Which control for which pest?

	ADHESIVE BARRIERS	BACILLUS THURINGIENSIS	HAND METHODS	DUSTING SULFUR	LIME SULFUR	PETROLEUM OILS	SOAP SOLUTION	WATER JET	MALATHION	METALDEHYDE	METHOXYCHLOR	NICOTINE SULFATE	PYRETHRUM	ROTENONE (CUBE)	RYANIA	SABADILLA
BURROWERS																
Borers	•		•													
Codling moths			•			•									•	•
Corn earworms			•						•						•	
Leaf miners			•						•					•		
LEAF CHEWERS																
Beetles	•		•										•	•	•	
Caterpillars	•	•	•										•	•		
Diabrotica			•						•		•				•	
Earwigs			•						•							
Grasshoppers			•													•
Japanese beetle			•												•	
Leaf rollers			•						•							
Oak moths		•	•													
Snails & Slugs			•							•						
Weevils			•													
NUISANCE INSECTS																
Ants	•		•						•							
Houseflies & Mosquitoes			•						•				•	•		
SOIL PESTS																
Cutworms			•													
Grubs & Wireworms			•													
Lawn moths		•	•										•	•		
SUCKING INSECTS																
Aphids						•	•	•				•	•	•	•	•
Leafhoppers												•	•	•	•	
Mealybugs						•						•				
Scale			•		•	•						•				
Spider mites			•	•	•	•	•	•							•	
Spittlebugs								•				•		•		
Thrips						•						•	•	•	•	
Whiteflies						•						•	•	•		

Pests ... and their telltale signs

A study of the more common garden pests illustrated below will help you to recognize them at first glance. The photographs on pages 34—35 will acquaint you with some of the helpful insects and small animals that can aid in controlling the more damaging invaders. Notice that beetles can fall into either category—helpful or harmful—and that earwigs are not all bad.

Many plant pests hide in the daytime, so if you see signs of damage, wait until dark, then go out with a flashlight to search for the marauders. You may see swarms of earwigs, slugs, or cutworms, and you can pick them off or eradicate them with a chemical spray right then. (For suggested chemical and non-chemical controls, see page 31.)

 Ants

Some kinds protect aphids, mealybugs, scale; feed on honeydew. Nests may injure plant roots. Some damage plants; others invade houses.

 Aphids

Tiny green, black, yellow or pink insects; sometimes winged. Live and feed in colonies; stunt plant growth. Some excrete honeydew; spread diseases.

 Beetles

Many kinds and sizes; feed on leaves, bark. Handpick large, slow-moving ones. Kill grubs (larvae) in the soil if you turn them up while cultivating.

 Borers

Many kinds; larvae (caterpillars or grubs) bore into stems and trunks. Paint adhesive on base of peach trees for peach borer.

 Caterpillars

Larvae of moths and butterflies; some smooth, others hairy; great variation in size and general appearance. Also see codling moth, borers. Most chew leaves.

 Codling Moths

The cause of wormy apples and pears. Larvae enter fruit as it starts to form. Spray after most petals fall; spray twice more at two-week intervals.

 Cutworms

Hairless moth caterpillars; common leaf-eating pests. Often cut off seedlings at ground level. Some feed at night, hide in soil during the day.

 Diabrotica

Also known as cucumber beetle; some closely related kinds are striped. Feed on many different vegetables and flowering plants. Larvae feed on roots.

 Earwigs

Night feeding insects. Feed on other insects as well as flowers and leaves. Check damaged plants at night, spray earwigs you find.

 Grasshoppers

Late summer pests with ravenous appetites. Most prevalent in warm winter, hot summer areas. Lay eggs in soil, hatch following spring.

 Grubs

Root-feeding beetle larvae that live just beneath soil surface. In lawns they feed on grass roots whereas lawn infesting cutworms feed on blades.

 House Flies

These don't damage plants. Good sanitation where garbage and garden wastes are stored, in dog runs and stables keeps them under control.

Lawn Moths

Larvae, called sod webworms, live near soil surface, eat grass blades at base. Adults, tan, inch-long moths, hover over lawns at dusk in summer.

 Leaf Miners

Insects lay eggs on leaf surfaces. Tiny larvae enter leaves; feeding results in unsightly serpentine effect. Spray to kill adults before they lay eggs.

 Leafhoppers

Small, fast moving green or brownish insects. Feed on underside of leaf causing white stippling on upper side. Some kinds spread virus diseases.

 Mealybugs

Small, white nearly immobile insects that form colonies at stem joints or toward base of leaves (usually the underside). House plants often attacked.

 Mosquitoes

Lay eggs on surface of still water; wigglers (larvae) live in water. Drain off water where it accumulates. Stock garden pools with fish.

 Oak Moths

Larvae eat leaves of western native oaks particularly in coastal California. Two broods each year — spring and summer. Larvae can strip tree leaves.

 Scale

Small insects that attach themselves to stems and leaves; generally covered with protective shell, form colonies. Some secrete honeydew, attract ants.

 Slugs, Snails

Among commonest, most destructive garden pests. Feed at night and on cool, overcast days, hide on warm, sunny days; leave a trail of silvery slime.

 Soil Mealybugs

Attach themselves to and feed on roots. Injury to roots interferes with water uptake; causes plants to wilt and die. Controls not too effective.

 Spider Mites

One of worst summer pests. Finely stippled leaves with silvery webs on underside; you need a hand lens to see the mites. One called red spider.

 Spittle Bugs

You can't see the bug because it's surrounded by protective froth. Feeds on stems, frequently on strawberries. Common, not-too-serious pest in spring.

 Thrips

Tiny, fast moving insects that damage plant tissue by rasping surface cells. Feed inside flower buds, so flowers seldom open. Also feed on foliage.

 Weevils

Many kinds including strawberry root weevil; most are quite small. Adults feed on leaves and fruit at night, hide by day. Grubs feed on roots.

 Whiteflies

Very small, common pests. Scalelike nymphs (young) attach to (and feed on) underside of leaves. Pure white adults flutter about erratically.

 Wireworms

Waxy, yellow, inch-long worms (grubs) cut roots, bore into bulbs, large roots, and stems, leaving irregular, deep pits. Also attack germinating seed.

A gallery of garden good-guys

Some plants, insects, and small animals will discourage or kill damaging pests. You can't always count on this kind of help, but you can learn which plants repel pests and which insects and animals you should protect and encourage to stay.

If you have a problem with nematodes (those destructive relatives of the ordinary earthworm), try interplanting marigolds with other flowers or vegetables. Once the nematodes get a taste of the plants' roots, they'll stay away from those planting areas. Some people think that another plant, *Euphorbia lathyrus,* has similar effects on pocket gophers; they dislike its bitter and poisonous roots.

Among the helpful insects, the most commonly found are lace-wings, mantids (the big praying mantis is the best known), ladybugs, stink beetles, and earwigs. You might also want to introduce a tiny and helpful wasp called *Trichogramma* to your garden. You just buy the eggs (advertised in many regional garden magazines), and place them in the garden; they hatch all by themselves.

Spiders eat lots of insects, and since some are nocturnal they can be working in your garden day and night. The most impressive looking is the enormous garden spider which spins a large and beautiful web.

Among the small animals, look for amphibians, (toads, frogs, and salamanders) and many kinds of lizards. They all do a good job of eating insects and other noxious creatures such as pillbugs. Some people may be lucky enough to have box turtles around to work on their slugs and snails.

You'll find that a great many birds feed on insects too. You can encourage them to remain in your garden by setting out suet in cold weather and providing a bath for them when it's warm. But be sure to keep the bath very clean or you may spread disease and kill off your helpers. Hummingbirds like to vary their nectar diet with some bugs. A well-stocked hummingbird feeder will keep them around.

If you don't mind their presence, the real garden-insect-eating champions are the shrew and the bat. The shrew is an above-ground relative of the mole. You will probably never see one, but you should hope that it's around. The bat is also a nearly invisible bug-gobbler. (You should never touch a bat or try to doctor a sick one, because they are apt to carry rabies.)

Some gardeners like to bring in ducks, bantam chickens, or even geese because they've heard that these birds eat slugs, insects and weeds. Unfortunately, they also love to eat good plants and dig holes.

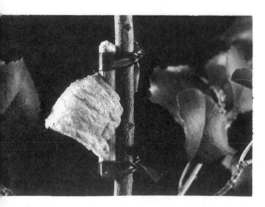

Lacewing egg *perches on its long fragile stalk. Compare the size of the egg with pencil point on the left.*

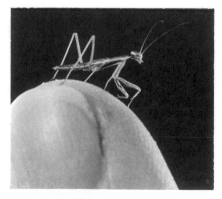

Hungry lacewing larva *kills many aphids by sucking out the juices, leaving only empty shells behind.*

Adult lacewing *has delicate light green coloring. Its only adult function is to lay more eggs before it dies.*

Mantis egg case *from a mail order house looks like brown froth. Tie it to stem of bushy shrub for egg hatching.*

Newly hatched mantis *is tiny, eats large quantities of aphids, scale insects, and other small pests.*

Large adult mantis *is seldom seen in garden. It eats larger insects; may lay countless numbers of eggs, then die.*

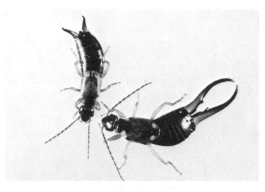

Female earwig is on left, male on right. Note that pincers are different shapes. Earwigs chew plants but also eat a lot of aphids.

Two-spot ladybug and its bristly larva both eat lots of small garden pests from the first warm weather until fall. Color of these little beetles ranges from nearly black to solid red.

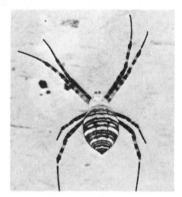

Wasp eggs of the genus Trichogramma are sold on a card. Tiny adult wasps destroy moth eggs. Big spider in photo at right is the orb weaver. It catches winged insects in its web.

Black beetle bites into a cutworm. These predators are often found climbing trees looking for food; they'll eat almost any insect they can catch, so don't kill them.

Marigolds help keep nematode worms away; plant them if these pests are a problem.

Tiny shrew, an aboveground relative of the mole, eats constantly, will even attack creatures bigger than itself. There are many species.

Suet feeder helps birds survive a cold spell. In spring they'll eat many bugs.

Suet placed in a pine cone gives birds the energy they need during winter. Cone looks natural in the garden. You can add a few seeds for omnivorous birds.

Hummingbird sips red sugar water from a feeder, also eats many small insects. These birds find the color red irresistible. Feeder attracts them to your garden.

Deer and other plant nibblers

A number of animals and birds can cause damage in the garden. Here are some suggested measures for protecting your plants against a few of these well known nibblers.

Birds. To protect seeds and seedlings from being eaten by birds, spread chicken wire or cheesecloth covers over the beds until the plants are full and sturdy. Check for any openings that will let the birds get through. To

protect fruit trees, throw a net over the whole tree. Either make your own of nylon netting, or ask if your garden supply store stocks a ready made kind. A less effective method is to hang reflectors, noise makers, or other fluttering objects from the tree's branches. Whatever protective measure you choose, keep in mind that many birds are omnivorous and help to control damaging insects.

Deer. Although they're nice to look at, deer can ruin the looks of a garden. To keep them away from your plants, use the following control methods: build chicken wire cages around young plants; build fences 6 to 8 feet high; use electric fences; scatter blood meal fertilizer or hang it up in small bags; spray strategic spots with mountain lion scent (available at nurseries); throw out moth balls; leave rags soaked in creosote in various spots; allow a deer-chasing dog to roam at night; use scarecrows or noisemakers. If none of these measures work, you can always resort to planting only those plants that deer dislike such as daffodils, holly, mahonia, rosemary, and zinnias.

Burrowing rodents. Rodents such as the pocket gopher and the ground squirrel can also cause enormous damage in a garden. The western rodent commonly called "gopher" is a vegetarian who nibbles at plant roots, eats plant tops and fruits such as pumpkins and melons, and piles up mounds of loose earth that may bury parts of plants he doesn't eat.

To catch a gopher, poke around until you find an opening to his underground tunnel. Then place a special two-pronged snap trap (available at nurseries or hardware stores) in the entrance. Tie the trap to a stake

Rosebushes disappear in a moment if a deer gets to them. Owning a big dog could help to discourage this muncher.

Viewed underground, a western pocket gopher eats a bulb. You can surround the bulb with wire to protect it.

or it may slide down the hole. Another way to keep a gopher and other tunneling rodents away is to put lighted road flares, gopher bombs, or chemicals (sold at nurseries) down the hole; some gardeners have even tried automobile exhaust. If the problem is serious, ask a professional exterminator for his help.

Some gardeners prefer to protect their plants with underground barriers. These can be as simple as lining each planting hole with chicken wire, or as complex as digging up an entire planting area and lining the bottom and sides of the cavity with wire.

Mice and voles. These tiny animals may or may not be annoying to gardeners. The population of voles (small, mouselike rodents) sometimes increases greatly overnight, and if your garden is in the way it may be damaged. Roaming cats can solve the problem if they like to hunt. Another method is to use poisoned grain in containers that have small openings that only a mouse or vole can enter. Sometimes mice will build up a resistance to this poison so they may turn up again shortly after you think you've solved the problem.

Moles. Considered insectivores instead of rodents, moles dig tunnels as they hunt for underground grubs and worms. As they push along, plant roots may be cut or damaged; whole plants may even be pushed out of the ground. If you see a mole hill, push the soil down firmly to close the tunnel and prevent plants from drying out at the roots. You can try catching moles with traps or baits, but since they use most runs only once, catching them is very difficult. And because the mole's permanent home is deep in the ground, it's unlikely that you'll be able to find it.

Rabbits and hares. Because they're especially fond of tender greens, rabbits and hares can be a terrible nuisance in the vegetable garden. A few cottontails can

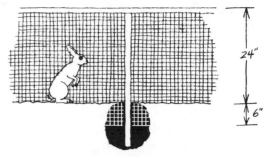

Rabbits are diggers. *Bury a piece of wire fence to keep them out of your garden. This may work with gophers too.*

nearly clear a vegetable patch in a very short time. The best solution is to build a fence of fine chicken wire with the bottom buried in a 6-inch-deep trench. Another effective method is to let a dog or cat roam around at night provided the animal is a hunter.

Squirrels. These rodents can strip nut trees bare overnight. They will also dig in flower pots. If you don't mind losing a few nuts and can keep your flower pots near your house, you may be able to ignore the problem. However, if the damage becomes too great (stripped bark, young tree growth destroyed), your neighbors are probably having similar problems. Call a local county agricultural office to see if they have a program for controlling these pests.

Common plant diseases

Some of the most common plant diseases and suggested solutions are listed below.

Powdery mildew. A bluish-white dust that appears on leaves and flower buds. *Solution:* Discard infected annuals; cut off affected parts of permanent garden plants.

Rust. Blisters form on leaves and scatter reddish or yellow spores. *Solution:* Remove infected leaves.

Black spot. Black spots appear on leaves. *Solution:* Discard badly infected plants.

Wilt. This disease lives in the soil and frequently attacks tomatoes. *Solution:* Plant wilt-resistant varieties.

Damping off. Newly sprouted seedlings develop a stem rot near the soil surface and fall over (or the seeds never sprout). *Solution:* Bake containers of soil before sowing seeds.

Peach leaf curl. Leaves on peach trees become misshapen and curled, eventually falling off. This interrupts the flower/fruit cycle. *Solution:* Spray peach trees with lime sulfur or fixed copper sprays in winter during a period of dry weather and before leaf buds swell.

Camellia petal blight. Camellia flowers turn brown. *Solution:* Pick off infected flowers and keep area around plant very clean.

Many of these diseases can be prevented if you follow the gardening practices given below:

1) Keep your garden free of weeds, fallen fruit, and dead flowers.

2) Control the insect population using the methods described on pages 28–35.

3) Replace plants that show signs of disease year after year. Before choosing a different plant, ask your nurseryman if he stocks disease-resistant varieties of the damaged plant.

4) Rotate your annuals from year to year because some disease organisms affecting certain plants can remain in the soil and ruin the same annual next year.

5) Water plants deeply and infrequently (except plants in containers, see pages 64–65), adding nutrients as they are required.

6) Give your plants the proper growing conditions. Don't put sun lovers in shaded areas; and don't crowd plants together—it cuts down on air circulation.

7) Remove annuals and vegetables after their normal growing season. Old and weak plants are especially prone to disease.

8) Burn or discard any diseased plants; don't put them in a compost pile.

STARTING PLANTS
...seeds, cuttings, T-budding, grafting

Just looking at a seed rack may prompt this kind of daydream: You can picture many flowers already in bloom and vegetables and herbs seem to sprout growth right there on the seed rack. This kind of daydreaming can be so pleasant that beginning gardeners are often unprepared to meet problems that may occur later on.

The illustrations below show you how to prepare and nurture a bed of flowering plants from seed. If you want cut flowers, you may prefer to plant in rows. Vegetables can be sown in rows or in special mounds as described on page 115. Before you rush to the store for seeds, however, look over the warnings and suggestions that follow. They'll help to make your daydreams come true.

In choosing seeds, first check the instructions on the package for correct planting times. Also check the information on annuals and perennials (see pages 98-103) for tips on planting periods for different regions and climates. Then, before you start preparing the seed bed, turn to the section on soil and soil amendments (pages 4-7). Tender seedlings require perfect conditions to grow quickly and well. Count on a week or two for the seeds to sprout and another period of sparse growth before growth fills in and becomes sturdy.

Prepare soil, *water it, then outline planting areas with gypsum, stakes, or string. Place tall plants at rear.*

Shake fine seed *in a can with corn meal or white sand; you can see where seed falls as you sow it in the bed.*

Sow seeds evenly, *then lightly press seed into soil with back of spade. Cover with thin layer of sifted compost.*

Use fine spray *to dampen surface, then don't water again until seeds sprout, unless weather is hot or windy.*

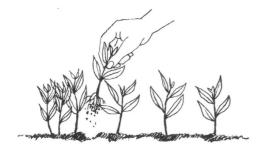

Transplant *or thin out beds when seedlings have two sets of leaves. Remove weeds when you recognize them.*

Irrigate *older plants with soaker. Allow 2 inches of soil to dry out before watering again. Feed only when watering.*

Starting seeds indoors

If spring weather in your area tends to be cold and wet you may want to get a head start with tender plants such as tomatoes and peppers, by starting them indoors. This method also protects the seedlings from possible attack by other living organisms until they become established. It will take about two months for the seedlings to mature enough so you can set them outside. If you sow them too early, the seedlings will be leggy and rootbound when planting weather arrives.

Use a commercial potting mix, or combine equal parts of light topsoil, fine ground bark or peat moss, and sand (sifted through a ¼-inch mesh screen). To kill any weed seeds and fungus in the soil, bake it in a hot oven for an hour before using.

Line a flat or other planting container with newspaper, slashing it to provide drainage holes. Then fill the flat with the soil mix until it is ½ inch from the top. To smooth out the surface, press down lightly using a piece of board.

Before planting the seed, check the package directions for recommended planting depth. You can cut planting furrows as shown below or scatter the seeds on the surface and sift a layer of soil on top. Then cover the soil with a dampened piece of newspaper.

The best way to water the seeds is to place the container in a sink or tub, add water to just below the seed level, and allow the soil to soak up the moisture until it is saturated. Drain the tub and let the container stand until well drained. Then place it in a warm spot, but not in direct sun.

After six days, begin checking daily for signs of sprouting. When the first sprouts appear, remove the paper and put the container in more light or filtered sun.

When the seedlings have developed two sets of true leaves, transplant them to 2-inch pots filled with moist planting mix. To do this, loosen the soil around each plant, gently grasp one of the leaves, and carefully pull out the seedling. Use a pencil to poke a hole in the new planting mix, drop in the seedling, and firm the soil around it. Keep the plants in the shade a day or two, then move them into the light again until ready to set out permanently.

Cut furrows in prepared flat, sow seed, cover with layer of soil. Plunge flat to seed level in a tub of water to soak.

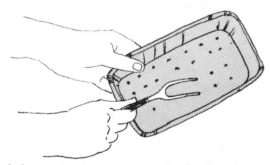

Poke holes in aluminum pan to make flat for a few seeds.

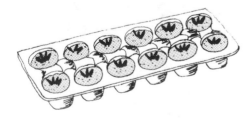

Egg cartons keep each seedling separate, hold water well.

Unroll seed tape in flat or in planting bed. Seeds are spaced on tape just the right distance apart. Water melts tape.

Seedlings came from seed tape. By the time they're this big the tape has dissolved. You can buy both vegetables and flowers in tape; plant in flats or in the ground.

Softwood cuttings

A common gardening dilemma: Your neighbor has geraniums that are just the right color for your patio, but you've never seen anything like them at the nursery. Or you visit a friend who has splendid azaleas, but she can't remember what variety they are. What can you do?

The answer is simple: Just ask your friend if you can take cuttings from these plants and start your own. All you need are a few branch tips. Wrap them in moist paper, then hurry home and set them in a special potting mix (see below).

You can take cuttings of new growth (called softwood cuttings) from late spring well into summer, beginning as soon as the spring growth is firm and sturdy. More mature cuttings will also root if you take them later in summer or early fall. Cuttings will produce plants exactly like those you took them from, whereas seeds may produce plants that are unlike their parents.

In choosing cuttings, look for normal, healthy growth; avoid fat or spindly branches. Softwood cuttings root best if you can snap them off cleanly from the parent plant. If they crush or bend, the wood is too old. If new leaves are still forming at the tip, the branch is too young for a cutting. Keep all cuttings cool and moist (not wet) until you can plant them.

ROOTING SOFTWOOD CUTTINGS

Fill a flat or pot with a blend of half sand and half pre-moistened peat moss, firming it down slightly so that the surface is a half inch below the top of the flat. Open a container of rooting hormone powder and place it beside the flat. One by one, remove the cuttings from their moist wrapping and make a clean, slanting cut with a razor blade or sharp knife just below a leaf or bud. If the leaves are very large, snip off about half of each leaf with scissors. Strip off any lower leaves so only the stem will be buried in the planting mix. Dip the stem in the hormone powder and tap it gently to remove any excess. Use a pencil to poke a hole in the sand and peat moss mixture and set in the cutting, firming the soil around the stem. When you've finished planting the cuttings, cover them with transparent kitchen wrap, a plastic bag, or a jar. Remove this cover once a day for a few minutes to allow air to circulate, then cover again.

If you can keep the temperature of the soil mix at 75 or 80 degrees (see discussion on next page), the cuttings will root more quickly. When new growth appears, the cutting has rooted. Gently lift one out, carefully removing some of the soil until you see roots. Then transplant the cutting to a slightly larger container to give the roots more growing room. Never move any plant from a tiny pot to a very large one. Use a size that allows for an inch or two of new soil around the root ball. When the new growth is full and sturdy, you can set the plants in the garden. Plants that cannot be set out when they're ready because of very hot or very cold weather may have to be transplanted to still another larger container to keep them from becoming rootbound.

SOME PLANTS TO TRY

The following list is by no means complete, but softwood cuttings from these plants will root fairly easily.

Perennials. Perennial alyssum, arabis, aubrieta, begonia, candytuft, chrysanthemum, dianthus (carnations, pinks), delphinium, geranium (includes ivy geranium, pelargonium), penstemon, sedum.

Woody plants. Azalea, bougainvillea, ceanothus, daphne, fuchsia, gardenia, heather, hibiscus, honeysuckle, hydrangea, ivy, lavender, oleander, plumbago, pyracantha, star jasmine, thyme, willow, wisteria.

How to root an azalea

Make clean cut at leaf node using knife or razor blade. Softwood cutting should be from new growth that is firm enough to snap off.

Insert cutting in hole made with pencil after dipping stem in hormone powder. Remove any leaves that would be buried in the soil.

Cover cutting with jar or plastic bag to create humidity. Lift once a day for air circulation, and to prevent mold from growing.

Check root growth when new leaves form. Azaleas may need 3 months to root. Transplant to slightly larger pot with acid soil mix.

A MINIATURE GREENHOUSE

If you fail to root softwood cuttings using the usual methods (see opposite page), try planting them in a plastic bag filled with perlite. You can use this miniature "greenhouse" for rooting house plants, perennials, shrubs, or trees.

Put two handfuls of perlite (a material available at nurseries) into a medium-sized plastic bag and wet it thoroughly. Then turn the bag upside down, keeping the neck loosely closed while you squeeze out the water. The perlite should be damp but not wet.

Prepare the cuttings as described on the opposite page and put the bare stem into the perlite. Then close the bag (to root succulents, leave it open) and put it in a spot that has good light but no direct sun. For air circulation, open the bag briefly each day but don't lift or disturb the cutting. It may take from a week to a month for the cutting to root. To test its progress, gently pull up on the cutting. If the perlite moves, there are roots running through it. Lift out the cutting and transplant it into a small pot or directly into the garden if weather permits.

Plastic bag *with moist perlite is good container for rooting softwood cuttings. The plastic holds in humidity.*

ROOTING FUCHSIAS IN A BAG

Although the method described below was developed for rooting fuchsias, it should work equally well for other cuttings taken from quick-rooting plants, such as ivy geranium or thyme. This method offers the great advantage of being able to handle a large number of cuttings while keeping them out of the way.

Fill a large, thick, plastic bag with a moist mixture of half sand and half peat moss. Use a strong cord to tie the bag closed, then hang it in a lathhouse, under a shaded and protected overhang, or in any other well lighted, wind-free place.

With a nail or ice pick, punch rows of holes in the bag from top to bottom, about 1½ inches apart. Then poke the stems of the cuttings into the holes using each row for cuttings of the same type. You won't need to water the sand and peat moss mixture (the plastic keeps the water in), but it doesn't hurt to mist the cuttings occasionally with water from an atomizer.

When the cuttings show new growth, move the bag to a work area and slit it between holes so that you can remove the cuttings without disturbing the new roots.

BOTTOM HEAT SPEEDS ROOT GROWTH

Softwood cuttings root more quickly if soil temperature remains constant at 75 or 80 degrees. If your house has radiant heating in the floors and you have only a few cuttings, you can just put them in an out-of-the-way corner and let the house heat do the job.

For a larger number of seedlings or cuttings you can use the age-old practice of laying a bed of fresh manure several inches thick in a coldframe (see pages 90 – 91) and setting the flats or pots on top. As the manure rots, it produces heat.

A third way to keep soil temperature constant is to use an electric coil heater. Most nurseries carry two different types. The best known is simply a long flexible coil that you wind around under your planting flats (see page 91). Different lengths of coil, or differences in materials, determine the price, but you should be able to find a coil heater for under $10. The other type of heating unit consists of a flat with the coil built in. These flats are about the size of an ordinary wooden flat and cost about the same as the more expensive coils.

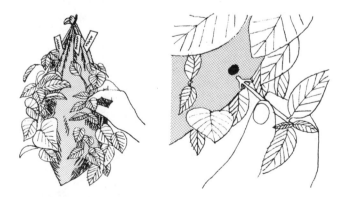

Punch holes *through plastic bag to insert cuttings. Make a separate vertical row for each kind of plant.*

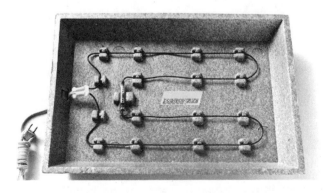

Electric heating cable *is held in place with clips attached to plastic flat; soil goes on top, stays warm.*

Hardwood cuttings

Certain deciduous shrubs and trees can be grown from cuttings taken in late fall anytime after the leaves have fallen but before the first frost. Such cuttings can take up to a year to root, so you'll need an out-of-the-way place to keep them until they take hold.

Some of the plants you can take cuttings from are deutzia, forsythia, grape, kolkwitzia, philadelphus, and weigela, as well as others with similar growth habits.

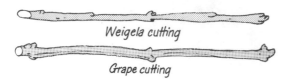

Weigela cutting

Grape cutting

Cuttings from most fruit and nut trees and big hardwoods, such as beech, birch, linden, maple, and oak, do not normally root. However, you can graft or bud fruit trees to start new varieties (see grafting and budding techniques on the opposite page and on pages 44 and 45).

CUT THEM PENCIL THICK

Cut off the tip of a selected branch at a point where it becomes about pencil thick. Discard the tip and cut off the next 6 to 9-inch section that includes at least two leaf buds; the end near the trunk should be cut on a slant just below a bud. Be sure to label each cutting before storing it.

TWO WAYS TO STORE

If your soil has good drainage in winter, dig a trench about two inches deeper than the thickness of the cuttings bundled together, lay them in it, and cover with dirt. If the ground is apt to freeze, cover the dirt with a mulch or with evergreen boughs if they're available.

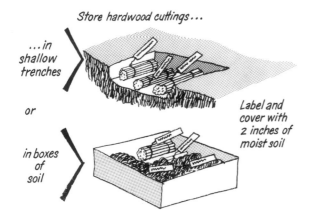

Store hardwood cuttings...

...in shallow trenches

or

in boxes of soil

Label and cover with 2 inches of moist soil

Another way to store cuttings is to place them in a box filled with moist peat moss. Keep the box in a cool place, making sure that the peat moss stays moist (not soaked) throughout the winter. The cut ends will callus over during the winter.

ROOTING HARDWOOD CUTTINGS

Because cuttings may take up to a year to root, start them in an out-of-the-way spot where they won't be disturbed. One way to do this is shown below. Place a bottomless box in a hole in the ground so that half of it is buried. Fill the container with sand up to ground level. Then set the cuttings in the sand so that an inch or so of each cutting is above ground. Then cover the box with a pane of glass. To protect the cuttings from direct sunlight, place a burlap-covered frame overtop. Keep the sand moist but not wet. When the cuttings have rooted and have enough full and sturdy growth, move them to their permanent spot. Keep them shaded until they become firmly established and begin to grow.

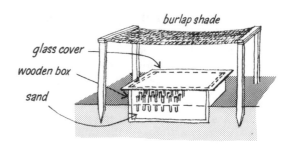

burlap shade

glass cover

wooden box

sand

LAYERING—A UNIQUE APPROACH TO CUTTINGS

Layering allows you to root a branch before you cut it from the parent plant. As shown in the drawings below, you cut halfway through a selected branch. Keeping the notch open with a pebble or matchstick, you then pin the notched section in a shallow hole, cover it with soil, and place a brick on top to keep the soil firm and hold the moisture in. Tie the remaining portion of the branch to a stake above ground. Perennials will root in 6 to 8 weeks; woody plants take up to 9 months. To test the rooting progress, remove the soil and pull up gently. If the branch is rooted, cut it off from the parent branch and plant elsewhere.

(For information on "air layering," see page 77.)

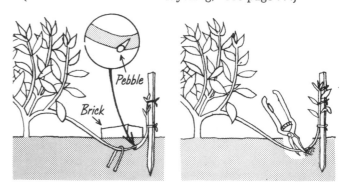

Pebble

Brick

Whip grafting

Grafting is a well known and ancient art. Many methods have been developed through the centuries; each has its followers. A number of the methods are somewhat difficult for the novice gardener. Below and on the following pages are three of the easier ones a beginner can try.

One of the most important reasons for grafting is to put a weak but desirable plant on a strong rootstock. Roses, fruit trees, walnuts, and grapes are often handled this way.

A home gardener will probably find grafting most useful for another purpose: You can make one fruit tree bear several varieties with different ripening times—perhaps once each month. This procedure also saves space and keeps the quantity of fruit in bounds. It often is used when a fruit tree (like a cherry) needs a pollinator. You can graft a branch of the pollinating variety onto the tree. It is even possible to graft several different kinds of fruit onto the same tree (apricots and plums for example) although not every mixture will take.

Grafting of deciduous trees and shrubs should be done before growth buds swell in spring. You can graft evergreens just before the surge of spring growth.

It's important to understand these three grafting terms: stock, scion, and cambium. The **stock** is the main plant that holds the graft. The **scion** (SIGH-un) is the new piece you graft to this stock. The **cambium** is the thin layer of tissue that lies between the bark and wood on both stock and scion. This tissue must be joined together for the graft to take, because all of a plant's nourishment passes through the cambium layer between root tip and twig tip.

To graft, you align a section of the cambium layer of the scion with the cambium layer of the stock (if the cambiums of stock and scion aren't perfectly aligned, the scion will dry up and die). Then nail or tape the two together. With bark grafting, shown on the next page, you would then trim off all but one strong graft after the scions begin growing. The whip graft method, below, does not require this trimming.

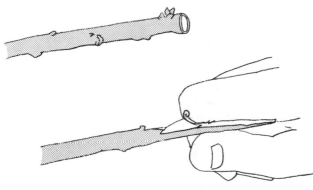

Apricot branch (top) is going into the plum business. It has just been cut back to a stub. A main diagonal slice will begin at right of the lefthand bud. Use a razor-sharp knife to cut an even diagonal, one thumb long. Trim the cut if necessary for an absolutely flat surface.

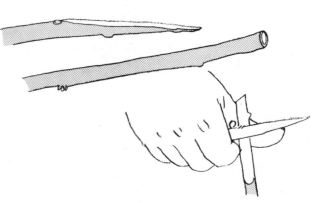

Scion (uncut branch above) should be same diameter as stock. Compare buds so when scion is cut to match stock, buds will point outward from tree, not inward. Then nick scion at beginning and end of cut so it will match the surface of cut stock as closely as possible.

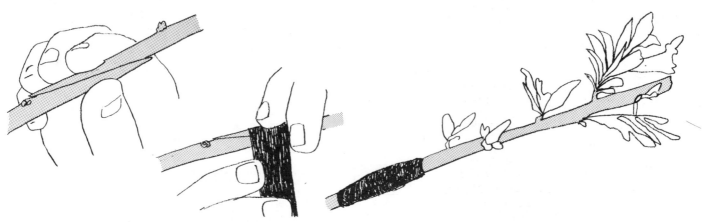

Place sliced face of scion against sliced face of stock to check fit. Bark edges should meet all around as shown above. Cut a 6-inch length of plastic electrical tape and wrap it around joint from middle to end; overlap ½ inch. Wrap second length from middle to other end.

Add 3 or 4 more layers of tape, winding tightly as you go. You can leave the tape in place permanently if graft takes, or remove it in third year. New shoots (as shown here) from plum buds show that the cambium layer was matched properly. The branch should bear fruit in the following year.

Bark grafting

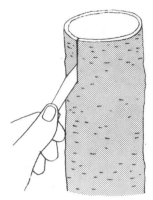
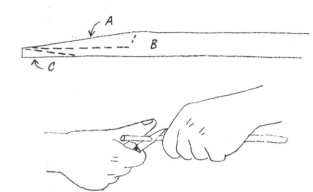
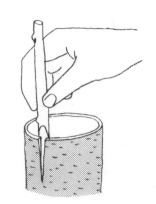

Make a slit for each scion. You can place 3 or 4 scions on the stock. Slice through stock bark to wood. Do bark grafting in early spring, when bark pulls away from wood easily. This means taking scions in winter and storing them in plastic bags in the refrigerator until spring.

Trim scions to fit into slit stock. Leave 3 or 4 buds on each scion. Make a slanting slice on inner side (A). In addition, you can cut a ledge at top of inner slice (difficult cut) to fit over stock (B), and also taper outer side so scion can slide under one flap of the bark (C).

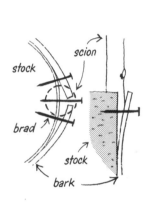
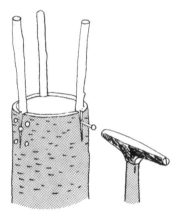

Lift bark and insert scion under one flap or down the middle—whichever makes the snugger fit (scions trimmed as shown in sketch at top of page will fit best under one flap). Drive a wire brad through the bark and scion into the stump. To make the scion really secure, drive brads through the flaps on each side of the scion.

Cover cut surfaces with grafting wax or asphalt emulsion grafting compound. All scions may not grow, but you probably wouldn't want to keep all anyway. How to train and select the growing scions is shown below. Until new growth begins, inspect grafting wax for splits; rewax any you find. In hot areas, whitewash the entire grafted tree.

If all scions are allowed to grow, this would become a weak crotch, subject to splitting...

So instead, train to one dominant branch, discourage all the others...

Discourage by pruning back unwanted branches at end of 1st year, leave selected branch alone

If only one scion grows, slice off dead shoulder on opposite side of stock

Follow these five basic steps: 1) Tie or tack 1 by 2-inch lath to stock as support for bark grafts. 2) This is why you should not leave all scions. 3) How one grafted branch takes over. Subdued branches have function—they help to heal graft. 4) How to encourage a branch, subdue others. 5) Remove dead shoulder on stock if only one scion takes.

T-budding

In whip and bark grafting, you burn your bridges behind you; the stock is cut whether the scion takes or not. When you propagate trees or shrubs by budding, you don't go to such extremes.

Nurserymen sometimes use T-budding to produce desirable varieties on a rootstock that grows easily from seed. They place a bud in the bottom three or four inches of a seedling. When they cut the stock, the growing part of the plant is the new variety.

You can bud in late summer, using trees or bushes with fairly thin, loose bark. Cut a **budstick** (a leafy branch with several buds at leaf bases) from the plant you want to propagate. Choose a one or two-year-old branch on the stock plant (the plant on which you'll place the bud) that is similar in size to the budstick.

Snip the leaves from the budstick but don't cut off the leaf stems. Use them as little handles for the buds you'll transfer. Continue with the budding operation following the illustrations below. After you finish budding, the leaf stems will be the indicators of success or failure. If

the stems wither and drop off but the buds remain plump and healthy, you have succeeded. If the entire bud shield or patch (bark, bud, and leaf stalk) withers or turns dark, you have failed.

In late winter, cut off the stock branch just above the new bud. The bud will sprout into a flourishing new branch in spring.

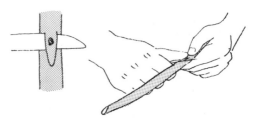

4. Slice under *a strong bud on the budstick, starting ½ inch below bud and finishing 1 inch above. You must cut down into the wood a bit, not just under the layer of bark.*

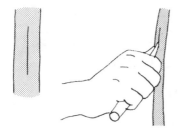

1. Make vertical cut *1 inch long in stock branch, slicing down to wood. Make the cut at the point where the stock branch is from ¼ to ½ inch in diameter.*

5. Remove shield-shaped piece *with bud by cutting it off about ¾ inch above the bud. Leave some of the wood attached to the back of the bark and bud.*

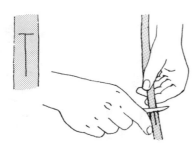

2. Make horizontal cut *through bark and into wood across top of the vertical cut. The horizontal cut should circle about ⅓ the distance around the stock branch.*

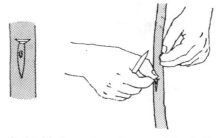

6. Push bud shield *down into loosened bark flaps of the stock, being careful not to damage the bud. Top of the shield should match the top of the T-cut on scion.*

3. Pry up *the corners gently. If the bark won't budge or chips away, it is too early or too late in the season for T-budding. To find out, try again in a week or two.*

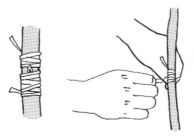

7. Bind the cut *with plastic electrical tape, leaving bud exposed. Don't use fabric tape, because it won't stretch. When the bud becomes a new branch, remove tape.*

NURSERY SHOPPING
...what to buy and how to buy it

The role of the nursery is to have the plants that you want on hand and to keep them in such a way that you can take them home and plant them whenever the proper planting season comes. Whether the nursery commodity is a leafy plant, a dormant plant, a seed, or a bulb, it is a living organism. The nursery industry has refined many ways of keeping and presenting these living organisms for you.

CHOOSING HEALTHY PLANTS

Wherever you buy your plants, seeds, or bulbs, the problem is the same as always: How do you choose the healthiest, strongest plant for your garden?

The first step is to find a nursery with conscientious employees who know their stock and can advise you. Ask friends and neighbors for their suggestions on where to go, and then try to do your shopping on off hours or off days when the pressure of business is light.

Following are a few things the inexperienced buyer should know.

Seeds. Seed racks are usually stocked with everything a given company produces for the year. But just because a package of seeds is there doesn't mean you can run home and plant the seeds. Don't buy anything until you read the directions on the package. Look for a date stamp. Is the seed meant for the current year? Look for suggested planting times (planting tomato seed in late June is wasted effort; the nursery probably has young plants).

Bulbs. For some reason, bulbs are sold out of season rather regularly. Check the bulb chart on pages 106–107 for proper planting times; don't buy them at other seasons.

Bedding plants and started vegetables. Bedding plants are all the flowering things that you use for a short and brilliant color display. They come in flats and a variety of small containers. You should buy young plants that will grow quickly after you plant them. Never choose those that are crowded or straggly. They've been around too long. You want compact plants with good leaf color and a few flowers in bloom. If you buy plants in individual plastic cells or containers, check the roots when you get home. Any long, white spaghetti at the bottom should be snipped off before planting. New roots will branch out into the soil. If you leave a coiled root on the plant, it may just go round and round under the plant, slowing or stopping growth.

Follow the same rule for vegetables, choosing compact plants with good color. A partial exception is tomatoes. Moderate stalkiness doesn't matter because you'll bury part of the stem when you plant. It sprouts roots underground.

Large containers. Plants in gallon and 5-gallon cans or corresponding plastic and pulp containers should be well branched with young and healthy looking bark and foliage. Although it's always a temptation to buy the largest plant you can afford, trees and shrubs often do better if you buy young-looking gallon-sized specimens and let them form their root systems in your garden.

If you're looking at fruit trees, roses, or other plants that are often sold bare root in fall and winter, ask how long the plants have been in the can. In the spring, nurserymen plant leftover bare root plants in cans. Such plants should grow in the can for several months before planting so that root growth will hold the soil together.

Common plant containers *found in the nursery:*
1) Plastic or metal 5-gallon can. 2) 2-gallon can.
3) Gallon can. 4) 15-gallon tree-sized can. 5) Bare
root tree. 6) Burlap-wrapped tree. 7) Papier maché
pots. 8) Bulbs. 9) Wooden flats of annuals.
10) Plastic pot. 11) Seeds. 12) 6-cell trays.
13) 6-plant tray.

Bare root material. See page 50 for details and kinds of plants to buy this way. Bare root material should have firm, moist stems and roots. If it is shriveled or dry and brittle looking, avoid it.

HOW TO TREAT YOUR PURCHASES

If the weather is hot, don't stop off to shop or visit on the way home leaving plants in the car. If you can get them home promptly to a cool and protected spot, you can wait a while to plant. But if you selected only a few plants that were taken from a nursery flat, they should be planted right away or they may dry out. Most plants should be planted in the early evening so that they can start their lives in the ground enjoying a relatively cool atmosphere.

Plants in flats should be pulled apart using slow pressure. This way, the roots remain more intact than they would if you sliced the plants out with a knife. Don't squeeze them or break up the soil more than you can help.

Plants in individual containers should have the outer surfaces of their root balls scratched so that roots will begin to grow outward soon after planting. A long, coiled root at the bottom of the root ball should be cleanly snipped off. A root that coils part way around the ball can be stretched outward as you plant.

If you can plant immediately, let the nurseryman cut the metal cans for you. Cans with corrugated sides need not be cut. Plants slide out easily. With small plastic containers, slide your hand over the soil surface with the plant stem protruding between your fingers; then turn the container over and tap it sharply. The plant should slide out. If it doesn't, water the plant and let it drain before trying again. Don't just yank. You may get the plant minus roots or dirt. Large plastic plant containers can be placed on their sides while you carefully guide the plant out.

If you can't plant bare root material right away, cover the roots with damp sawdust or peat moss or lay the plant in a shallow trench, covering the roots with a little soil.

SPECIALTY NURSERIES AND OTHER SOURCES

If you're lucky, you may have some specialty nurseries nearby that have an extensive collection of specific plants. There are rose nurseries, heather nurseries, begonia nurseries, and so forth. Their owners are usually dedicated gardeners who are nice to talk to and wise in the ways of plants.

Another source of good plants, often at low prices, are garden club or arboretum sales. You may find unusual plants that most nurseries don't offer and a lot of other gardeners who are eager to exchange gardening ideas.

Finally, there are mail order catalogs offering material ranging from odd seeds and imported bulbs to fruit trees and almost anything else you can imagine. Even if you never order a twig, these catalogs are pleasant to riffle and dream through.

PLANTING TECHNIQUES
...getting your trees, shrubs off to a good start

The methods for planting large shrubs and trees vary, depending on whether you buy a plant in a container, in a burlap wrap, or in bare root form. On the following pages you'll find the many planting and transplanting techniques for shrubs and trees and for special plants such as citrus and water lilies.

Container plants

If you choose a container plant from a reputable nursery, it is likely to do well, but one fact about a plant in a can is very important. Remember that it was started as a container plant. The soil is probably a special light mix that is unlike your garden soil. If you just dig a hole and drop the plant in, it may never root outside the nursery soil mix. The soil difference creates a barrier.

To prevent this, take the following steps (see page 13 for illustrations of this process): 1) Dig a hole twice as wide as the root ball and half again as deep (if the removed soil is very dry, soak the hole before planting). 2) Rough up the bottom and sides of the hole, then add a little organic material and some superphosphates to the bottom soil (for the amount of superphosphate, follow label directions). 3) Mix the soil you removed with more organic material—2 parts soil to 1 part organic matter. 4) Use this soil mixture to fill the hole about halfway up. Set the plant in and, if needed, add more soil until the top of the root ball is level with the ground. 5) Continue adding soil until the hole is filled. 6) Form a watering basin with leftover soil. 7) Water thoroughly.

Carrying two cans: *Put thumb in one, index finger between, remaining fingers in other; or use special tool.*

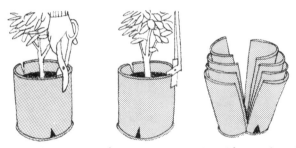

Cut cans *from top to bottom on opposite sides, using tin snips or can cutter. Stack empty cans for easy handling.*

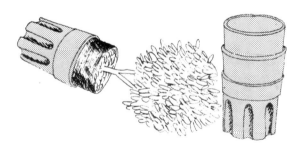

Corrugated cans *(at left) and smooth plastic cans need no cutting. Tap the bottom, then pull stem gently.*

Choose plants *that are full and young looking like the one on the left. Dense plant at right may be rootbound.*

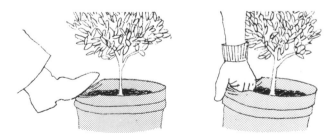

Single can *is easier to carry if you kick down the rim to form a handle. Wear gloves to prevent cuts and scrapes.*

Roots that circle *the root ball must be pulled loose. Use stick or tool to lift them, but don't break soil ball.*

Balled and burlapped

In fall and early winter, large shrubs and trees often are sold at nurseries with their roots wrapped in burlap. Balled and burlapped plants have a distinct advantage over container plants; they are never root bound. Among the plants sold this way you may see the following:

CONIFERS. Arborvitae, Cedar, False cypress (*Chamaecyparis*), Fir, Juniper, Pine, Spruce, and Yew.

EVERGREEN SHRUBS. Azalea and rhododendron, Boxwood, Daphne, Holly, Mountain pieris (*Pieris japonica*).

DECIDUOUS PLANTS. Azalea, Beech, Dogwood, Liquidambar, Magnolia, Maple, Tuliptree (*Liriodendron*).

As you move burlap-wrapped plants from the nursery to their planting sites in your garden, be careful not to break up the root ball or let it dry out. The best way to carry a plant is with both hands under the root ball. If it's too heavy for you to handle alone, shift it onto a piece of canvas or tarp and ask a friend to help you move it (see step 1 below).

If you can't plant it right away, put it in a shady spot, covering its root ball with moist organic material such as sawdust or peat moss.

You should normally stake a balled and burlapped plant because the root area is round and can act like a ball and socket joint, turning in the wind. If it shifts, the new roots will break and the plant will not grow. Be sure to position the stake before you fill the hole with dirt so you don't run it through the root ball.

It isn't necessary to unwrap the plant entirely (see step 3). The burlap will rot away eventually.

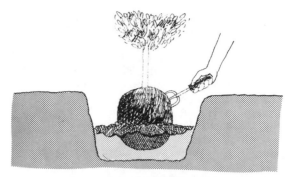

3. Add some soil, *cut twine, lay back burlap. Scrape ball gently if you see a crust. Leave burlap in place.*

4. Firm soil *when hole is half full so root ball will not settle below the ground level after plant has been watered.*

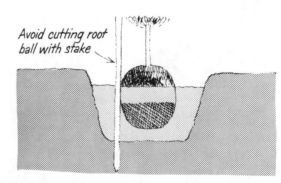

Avoid cutting root ball with stake

5. Drive stake *so that it's anchored in firm soil and rests against (but does not damage) the root ball.*

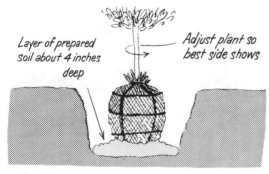

1. Ask a friend *to help you carry a balled and burlapped plant on a tarp or piece of canvas to planting site.*

Layer of prepared soil about 4 inches deep

Adjust plant so best side shows

2. Set root ball *in a hole that is twice the width of the root ball and 4 inches deeper than the height.*

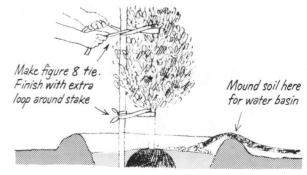

Make figure 8 tie. Finish with extra loop around stake

Mound soil here for water basin

6. Tie trunk *securely to stake (not too tightly). Flood watering basin several times to soak soil very deeply.*

Buying bare root-economical, sensible

Bare root planting is a method—and usually the best method—of planting deciduous plants (those that lose their leaves in winter, such as roses, apples, or sycamores). Commercial growers raise the plants to salable size in their growing fields. Then in early December, they dig up the plants, clean and trim the roots, and ship the plants off to retailers.

Normally, bare root plants are sold from bins of wet shavings or earth. Sometimes you can find bare root plants being sold with their roots covered with fancy wrapping. Some nurserymen put bare root plants into containers as soon as they receive them, but will bare the roots again if you ask them to.

Here are some tips for buying and planting bare root deciduous plants. Following these suggestions is a listing of the many kinds of trees and shrubs (in addition to roses) that you can buy and plant using the same techniques discussed below.

Two valid reasons for buying and setting out a bare root plant in winter or early spring rather than waiting until spring, summer, or fall when you can buy the same plants in containers, are the following: 1) You save money. Typically a bare root plant costs only 30 to 70 percent of what the same container plant will cost later in the year. 2) The manner in which a bare root plant is planted makes it easier to maintain, often makes it grow faster, and makes it healthier and more vigorous than a container plant would be if set out later in the year.

When you plant a bare root tree, the soil you use to refill the planting hole does not have to be amended as it would for container plants. But, if your garden soil is so bad that you feel you must add an amendment, be sure to improve the whole area into which the roots of the mature plant will spread (about the same width of soil as the width of the mature top growth). When planting bare root material, use the same techniques as shown in the photographs on the opposite page.

For bare root planting to be successful, the roots should be fresh (not half dead) and plump (not dry and withered), and in many cases the roots and tops should be pruned according to the kind of plant. For these reasons you should buy your bare root plants (packaged, or out of bins of shavings) from a nursery and not from a store that sells nursery plants as a sideline. Only an experienced nurseryman is likely to keep bare root plants in such a way that their roots will be fresh and plump when they are sold. And only an experienced nurseryman will know how to prune the tops and roots of the plant you are buying and will be able to give you accurate and specific advice about how and where to plant it.

If you have any doubt about the freshness of the roots, soak them overnight in a bucket of water before planting.

Following is a list of some of the many plants sold bare root:

FRUIT TREES: apple, apricot, peach, plum.

NUT TREES: almond, filbert, walnut.

OTHER FRUITS: blackberry, blueberry, grapes, raspberry.

SHADE TREES: ash, beech, birch, box elder, catalpa, horse chestnut, linden, maple, oak, poplar, sycamore, tulip tree, weeping willow.

FLOWERING PLANTS: bittersweet, cherry, crabapple, dogwood, forsythia, honeysuckle, lilac, plum, quince, spiraea, viburnum, weigela, wisteria.

Bare root plants are kept in damp shavings or soil until they are sold. Have roots, tops trimmed when you buy.

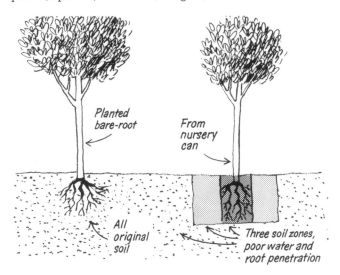

Planted bare-root

From nursery can

All original soil

Three soil zones, poor water and root penetration

Soil surrounding bare root plant on left doesn't need amendments, but container plants require amended soil.

How to plant a bare root rose

1. Dig hole *to fit trimmed roots just before spring growth begins. Form cone of soil in the bottom.*

2. Spread roots *evenly over cone-shaped soil at 30° angle. Snip off extra long roots so 18 inches is left.*

3. Use shovel handle *to place plant so first branch is just above ground (or just below if ground freezes).*

4. Add soil *gradually, firming it around the plant with your feet; straighten the plant with each soil layer.*

5. Slowly water *around plant before you finish filling to ground level, soaking soil deeply. Let water drain.*

6. Cover plant *with loose soil or peat moss until growth begins; at that time form watering basin and soak deeply.*

A better way to plant eucalyptus

Since eucalyptus is evergreen, it's not sold in bare root form. However, because a container eucalyptus is always root bound you should turn it into a bare root plant before planting.

Carefully remove the soil from the roots, then wash them clean. Spread the roots apart so they point outward from the center.

Prepare a hole as you would for bare root planting (see photographs above), making it large enough to contain all the roots. If you have to clip some roots off, trim back the top growth too. Place the plant on a mound of soil in the planting hole so it sits at the same level as it did in the container. Poke a stake into the soil next to the trunk; be careful not to damage any roots. Then loosely tie the tree to the stake with a figure-8 tie so it can sway a bit in a wind. Fill the planting hole and water deeply.

Wash off roots *of eucalyptus taken from a nursery can, then carefully spread them apart; clip off broken ones.*

Moving a shrub

The photographs on this page illustrate an easy way to move a shrub. All you need is chicken wire and a tool to twist the wire (a hook, pliers or big screw driver). This method will work for most normal sized shrubs; however, if your plant measures more than 2½ feet, it's best to get the assistance of a landscape contractor. In mild climates, most shrubs can be moved in early fall. In cold climates, wait until after the last frost.

To lessen the shock of transplanting, sink a spade to its full depth in a circle around the plant just under the outermost leaves (called "drip line") about a month before you transplant. The roots you cut will form branching rootlets that help the plant to reestablish itself after you transplant.

Just before transplanting, dig a broad trench just *outside* the dripline. Dig as deep as the root ball is wide. Then wrap the root ball with wire and tighten as shown in the photo at upper right. Finally, slice under the ball with your spade.

In most soils the wire should help to keep the bottom soil intact as you remove the shrub; for very crumbly soil, slide a length of wire under the plant.

1. Dig trench *around plant directly below outside branches. Trench must be wide enough so you can wrap root ball.*

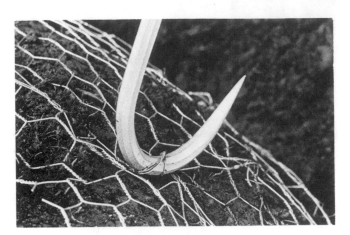

3. Place hay hook *or other tool through wire and twist tightly. Do this at 4 or 5 places and at different levels.*

2. Wrap root ball *(a foot or more deep) with length of chicken wire, securing the loose ends.*

4. Cut under root ball *with mattock or shovel. If earth crumbles, slide chicken wire underneath to keep intact.*

Mild winters? Plant in fall

Wherever winters are fairly mild, shrubs, trees, ground covers, and even some herbaceous plants will get a head start if you plant in fall. But if you're likely to have cold periods or even just a hard frost or two, be sure the plant is a kind that withstands cold.

For this technique to work properly, you must set out the plants early enough so the soil remains warm while they begin to root. Late September or early October is about the right time. Try any of the plants listed in the next column.

ANNUALS AND VEGETABLES: Calendula, Iceland poppy, nemesia, pansy and viola, primrose, snapdragon, stock, pea family, cabbage family, other early bloomers.

PERENNIALS: Any that flower in spring or early summer.

SHRUBS: Azalea, camellia, ceanothus, conifers, daphne, privet, rhododendron, roses, lilac, native shrubs.

TREES: Use any that are not tender in cold weather.

GROUND COVERS: Chamomile, mondo grass, rosemary, strawberry, star jasmine, ice plant.

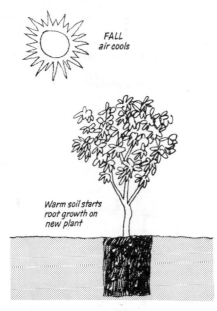

Warm soil *forces root growth, but mild fall air temperatures won't wilt or burn the plant's foliage.*

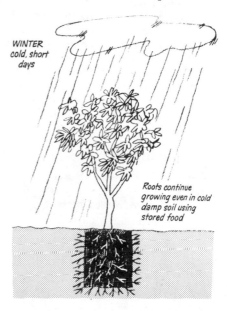

Rain waters *the plant, and root growth continues into cold weather, even after the soil has cooled.*

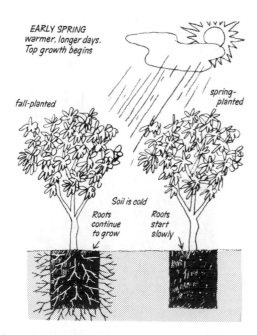

Fall planted shrub *on left is well rooted while its spring-planted neighbor gets slow start in cold soil.*

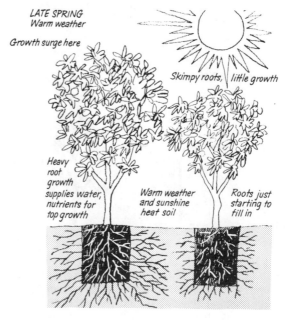

Warm weather *brings top growth on rooted plant, but spring-planted one has too few roots for big spurt.*

A living fence–with hedge plants

You may think of a hedge as just another kind of fence or wall—one with many drawbacks: It grows and fills in slowly, it requires constant maintenance, and it needs to be fed and watered.

A hedge, however, offers many advantages that a constructed barrier can't match. For example, in a small garden, a barrier of living plants is more pleasing to the eye than a wooden or masonry wall. It continues the effect of the garden instead of bringing it to a full stop. And a hedge can be used to define areas. For example, plant a low border around paving.

A hedge can be any line of suitable plants you choose to use as a barrier. It might be a squared-off, 4 to 6-foot wall of privet or boxwood, a row of clumping bamboo in front of a dog run, or a soft low border of English lavender around a bed of perennials. You can shear a hedge to maintain a particular shape, trim it once or twice a year for a natural effect, or just use plants that tend to grow to a certain size or shape without much care or training. On the opposite page you'll find a listing of plants that can be used as a hedge. Whatever plant you choose, don't choose one that's rangy or fast-growing, thinking that you'll be able to control its growth by frequent shearing. Most likely it will get out of hand.

For a formal hedge, all plants must be the same kind or you will spoil the effect. A natural screen, however, often can consist of predominantly one kind of plant plus a few others that flower or have different foliage.

A formal hedge requires different planting techniques, training, and maintenance than a natural, varied one. Set out the plants 18 inches apart. Shear from 2 to 6 inches off the top at the start, and several times every growing season. Trim the sides less severely until the plants spread to the width you want, then maintain that size.

For a natural hedge, place plants about 3 feet apart and then let tops grow naturally. Trim the sides once or twice a year or as necessary. A low border hedge will require closer spacing because the plants are smaller.

Use care in spacing

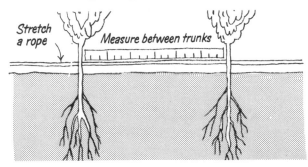

Stretch a rope to plant straight hedge. Measure from trunk to trunk for even spacing. For tall hedges, space plants 18 inches apart; for low border, 12 inches apart.

Hedges need haircuts

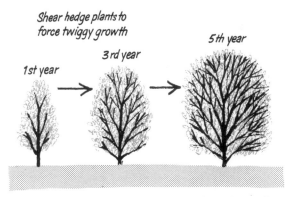

Trimming of formal hedges should be done from the time you plant. To force dense, twiggy growth, clip young plants 2 to 6 inches at top and 2 inches or more on sides several times each growing season. When the hedge reaches desired height, trim frequently, always cutting at an angle as shown in the sketch at right. This will allow sun to reach the bottom and force dense leaf growth.

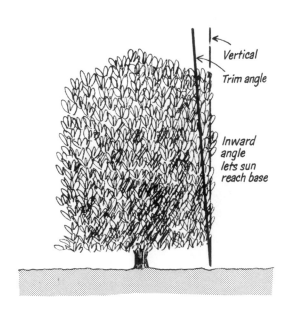

For curved hedge, use a hose to form the line, then keep it in place with stakes. Cut along hose with spade, move the stakes and hose 18 inches; then dig trench.

In the list below, the following abbreviations are used: E (evergreen), D (deciduous), Low (up to 18 inches), Med (1½ to 5 feet), Tall (5 to 10 feet or more), S (will stand shearing), N (natural growth habit only).

Acacia	E • Tall • N
Atriplex	E,D • Med, Tall • S,N
Bamboo	E • Low, Med, Tall • N
Berberis	E,D • Low, Med, Tall • S,N
Buxus (Boxwood)	E • Low, Med, Tall • S,N
Camellia japonica	E • Med, Tall • S,N
Ceanothus	E • Med, Tall • N
Chaenomeles (quince)	D • Med, Tall • N
Choisya (Mexican orange)	E • Med, Tall • N
Cotoneaster	E,D • Med, Tall • S,N
Elaeagnus pungens	E • Med, Tall • S,N
Euonymus	E,D • Low, Med, Tall • S,N
Garrya elliptica	E • Med, Tall • N
Ilex aquifolium (holly)	E • Med, Tall • S,N
Ilex cornuta (holly)	E • Med, Tall • S,N
Ilex crenata (holly)	E • Low, Med, Tall • S,N
Laurus nobilis	E • Tall • S,N
Lavender	E • Low, Med • S,N
Leptospermum	E • Med, Tall • S,N
Ligustrum (privet)	E,D • Med, Tall • S,N
Nerium oleander (oleander)	E • Med, Tall • N
Osmanthus	E • Med, Tall • S,N
Pachistima myrsinites	E • Low, Med • S,N
Photinia	E,D • Tall • N
Pittosporum	E • Med, Tall • S,N
Podocarpus	E • Med, Tall • S,N
Prunus caroliniana	E • Tall • S,N
Prunus ilicifolia	E • Med, Tall • S,N
Prunus laurocerasus	E • Tall • S,N
Prunus lyonii	E • Med, Tall • S,N
Pseudotsuga menziesii	E • Tall • S
Punica granatum 'Nana'	D • Low, Med • N
Raphiolepis indica	E • Med • N
Rhamnus alaternus	E • Tall • S,N
Rosa (rose)	D • Med, Tall • N
Rosemary	E • Low, Med • S,N
Santolina	E • Low • S,N
Sequoia sempervirens	E • Med, Tall • S
Tamarix	E,D • Tall • S,N
Taxus (yew)	E • Med, Tall • S,N

Some specialties...

Some plants require special care in planting in order to do well. Citrus, for example, is sensitive to moisture and must not be planted too deeply. Acid-loving, shallow-rooted plants such as camellias, azaleas, and rhododendrons require extra organic matter added to the soil and a wide shallow hole for their wide fibrous roots.

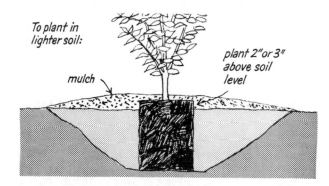

Camellias, rhododendrons, azaleas. *Make planting hole twice width of root ball; plant slightly high. If soil is heavy clay, plant with half of root ball above soil level and heap mulch around it. Always use light soil mix.*

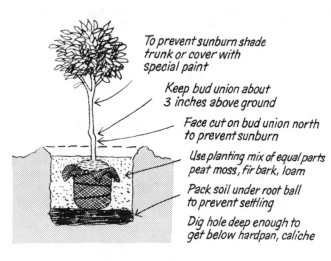

Citrus. *Most varieties are susceptible to damage from over-watering. Keep the plants away from lawns. If your area is likely to have late frosts, the plants must be covered with paper or burlap or kept under protective overhang.*

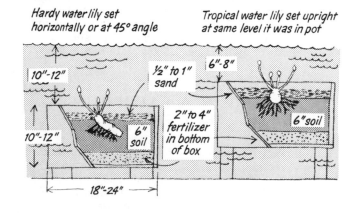

Water lilies. *Plant these, other aquatic plants in containers that can be submerged and taken out for replanting every 3 years. Plant hardy types in spring. Plant tropicals when the weather and water temperatures warm up.*

LAWNS AND GROUND COVERS
...putting them in, keeping them green

To some homeowners, nothing will ever take the place of green grass. No other surface feels so good under bare feet and serves as well for tumbling, wrestling, playing catch, or for spirited games of croquet or badminton. Even in the arid southwestern states where summer rains are meager or nonexistent, gardeners are willing to water, feed, mow, and cope with weeds in order to enjoy the pleasures of a lawn.

WHAT CONSTITUTES A LAWN?

Most people think a lawn should consist of grass, and a large proportion of this group believes that bluegrass is the only *real* lawn grass. This belief is understandable if you live in the northern regions of the country where the summers are cool and wet—the climate in which bluegrass evolved. However, from California through Texas to the Carolinas, a good lawn is likely to be composed of a subtropical grass like Bermuda, zoysia, St. Augustine, or even dichondra, which isn't a grass at all but a creeping plant with stems and round leaves.

Whatever the type, a lawn is a planted surface that should be able to withstand relatively heavy traffic without dying.

IS YOUR SOIL ACID OR ALKALINE?

Occasionally you'll find a soil that is so acid or alkaline that nothing will grow in it. Acid soils generally occur in rainy climates, alkaline soils in arid regions. If you suspect that your garden soil is one way or the other, send a sample of it to a soil testing laboratory (ask your county agricultural agent to recommend one). The sample should consist of several trowelfuls of soil taken from different spots in your garden, then mixed together. Use a trowel to do the mixing. If the results show you have acid soil, you can improve it by mixing in a layer of ground dolomite limestone at 50 to 75 pounds per 1,000 square feet. To improve alkaline soils, use 35 to 50 pounds of gypsum per 1,000 square feet.

PUTTING IN A LAWN TO BE PROUD OF

The following pages illustrate a step-by-step method for sowing a lawn properly. If you follow the directions carefully, you'll have far less trouble keeping it healthy. Before you start the job, consider the following points:

1) If your present lawn consists of weeds and crabgrass, the sod should be removed completely. You can rent power cutters that cut sod into strips, or you can use a flat spade to scrape it off. Don't turn any of the sod into your soil.

2) Don't add new topsoil unless you want to raise the level of the lawn. If so, make sure you mix about half of the topsoil into the ground before adding the rest; otherwise the sharp difference in soil quality will create a barrier against water penetration and root growth.

REAPING WHAT YOU SOW

The excitement and satisfaction of watching those first blades of grass grow into a solid carpet of green will be reward enough for the time and hard work involved in preparing the soil and sowing the grass seeds. But the job doesn't end here. You'll need to keep the grass properly fertilized (see pages 60 and 61) and you'll need the proper tools for cutting and raking.

The four traditional types of lawn mowers are the push reel mower, the gasoline-powered reel mower, the gasoline-powered rotary mower, and the electric rotary mower. Generally, push reel mowers are adequate for most small lawns, but for larger areas a power reel mower lends a big hand. Hand or power reel mowers do a better job of cutting grass very short, while power rotary mowers do a better job of cutting grass at taller heights; they are also good for cutting weeds. (Some professional gardeners prefer to use the more expensive forward-throwing power reel mower; it does an excellent job of cutting wet grass.)

Other lawn tools and equipment you may find useful are trimming shears, an edger with a long handle, a sturdy rake, and a large square of canvas for removing and transporting leaves and clippings.

MOWING TECHNIQUES

Bermuda and zoysia lawns require frequent mowing to within ½ inch of the soil surface—otherwise grass runners may become a problem. Lawns composed of cool climate grass, such as bluegrass or bent grass, are usually left longer—up to 2 inches. If you're unsure of the cutting height for your grass, get the advice of a professional gardener or nurseryman in your area.

Before mowing grass, make sure it is dry enough so that your mower will not dig into the turf or leave tracks. If you have to mow wet grass, drag a piece of burlap or a section of hose across the surface to remove excess moisture.

1. Remove old turf with a power sod cutter or a flat spade. Roll up the strips and discard them. Don't dig in any remnants; they'll spoil new lawn.

2. Spread soil amendment, superphosphate. Use calcium cyanamide to kill weed seed and supply nitrogen, but wait 30 days before sowing seeds.

3. Till soil with a rotary tiller, cutting 6 to 9 inches deep and crossing several times at right angles for a thorough and even mix of soil and additives.

4. Clean up sticks, stones, and roots, then use your hand to check soil here and there to make sure there are no clods or pockets of amendment.

5. Install permanent sprinklers at this point, using temporary long risers for heads until the lawn surface has settled and grass is well started.

6. Drag surface with board scraper (any version of the types shown here) to level high spots and fill in depressions. Firm surface with light roller.

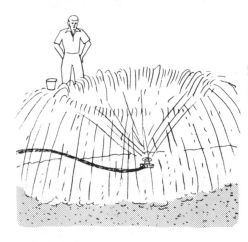

7. Water the surface for an hour or more to settle the soil and start the calcium cyanamide (see step 3) working on weeds. Water for 30 days.

8. Sow radish seeds (quick to sprout) to make sure calcium cyanamide has worn off. If seeds sprout, soil is safe. Pull up radishes, level ground again.

9. Use light roller to firm and smooth soil. The soil should be dry before rolling, otherwise it compacts, preventing seeds from sprouting.

(Continued on next page)

10. Spread fertilizer *(one with phosphorus and potassium) for good root growth of new lawn. Calcium cyanamide (see step 3) supplied nitrogen.*

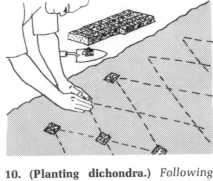

10. (Planting dichondra.) *Following pattern shown here, cut 2-inch squares from flats and place them 6 to 12 inches apart, level with surface.*

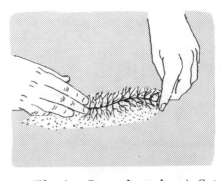

10. (Planting Bermuda stolons.) *Cut shallow trenches 10 inches apart and place the stolons as illustrated; or, broadcast like seed, then roll, mulch.*

10. (Planting sod.) *Lay strips so joints are uneven (like pattern for running bond brick), then roll to press roots into soil and water thoroughly.*

10. (Planting seed.) *Divide the quantity in 4 portions, then carefully sow each portion of seed going first north to south, then east to west.*

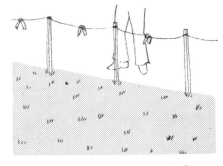

11. Rake surface *lightly to even seed, then rake again at right angles. Scatter any dense concentration of seeds with your rake but don't gouge soil.*

12. Scatter organic mulch *(⅛-inch layer) over seed or stolons. If you use peat moss, moisten it well before you start or it won't absorb water.*

13. Roll mulch *with a light roller, walking carefully with soft-soled shoes so you don't leave heel marks. A flat-footed walk helps avoid marks.*

14. Place string barrier *to remind passersby that seed is sprouting. Keep it in place about 3 months or until turf becomes firmly established.*

15. Hand water *using soft spray several times a day to keep soil moist but not saturated. Areas that dry out between waterings may not sprout seeds.*

16. Use plank *to pull up any weeds before they have time to shade out grass. Don't leave the plank on the seed bed or it will kill the seedlings.*

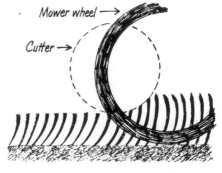

Mower wheel →

Cutter →

17. Mow grass *when it is tall enough to bend slightly (about 1 to 2 inches). Use a sharp, well aligned mower, cutting about ½ inch of grass blades.*

Dealing with weeds

The term "weed" can be applied to any undesirable plant you find growing in your lawn. For example, you may enjoy the early spring appearance of the English daisy dotting the grass, whereas other gardeners might feel it spoils the even texture they would like to have. If you follow the school of thought that a lawn should consist solely of grass, read on.

Lawn weeds should be removed before they have a chance to spread. The two ways to do this are to pull them up by hand or with a tool, or use a chemical spray.

Two effective weeding tools are the screwdriver and asparagus knife. If the lawn is moist, these tools will help you to pry out deep-rooted weeds such as dandelions and plantain, or to lift up weed runners like those on bur clover.

Below you'll find recommended chemical controls for the common lawn weeds along with some suggestions on how to maintain your lawn to prevent weeds from growing.

Crabgrass. A hot weather annual, crabgrass sprouts in the spring and vigorously spreads its wide leaves, crowding out other grass. When cool fall weather arrives, it turns reddish brown, then dies, leaving its seed in your lawn.

Hairy crabgrass *has broad leaves and runners.*

One effective non-chemical method for controlling crabgrass is to set your lawn mower at a higher setting; the taller grass prevents sunlight from reaching the crabgrass seeds. A second way is to avoid wearing lawn grass down to bald spots so crabgrass can get a foothold. A third way is to water the lawn infrequently and deeply. The lawn surface will stay fairly dry, cutting down seed germination.

A chemical control for crabgrass is to apply a product containing azac, balan (benefin), betasan (bensulide), or dacthal in winter. Then if any crabgrass sprouts in spring, treat it with a chemical containing amine methyl

Smooth crabgrass *has narrow leaves and runners.*

arsonate, disodium methyl arsonate, or calcium methyl arsonate. Although these chemicals may initially change the color of your grass, this condition is only temporary. Be sure to water the area thoroughly before applying any of the chemicals listed above, then give the grass a second treatment a week later.

Bermuda grass. In hot climates, Bermuda grass grows better than cool season grasses (bluegrass and bent grass). You can encourage its growth by setting your lawn mower at a low setting. This practice weakens other grasses and encourages growth of Bermuda. The only way to kill Bermuda chemically is to apply dalapon to the entire patch of Bermuda repeatedly. Handle dalapon with care because it also kills desirable lawn grasses.

Quackgrass. In cool climates, quackgrass spreads by rhizomes (underground stems that root). Quackgrass also spreads seed heavily; some of the seeds sprout quickly while others lie dormant for years. In addition, quackgrass poisons other grasses.

At the first sign of quackgrass, treat the infected areas with a chemical called amino triazole. If quackgrass gets out of hand you may have to have a professional sterilize the ground with a fumigant or sterilant (ask your nurseryman for the name of a contractor who does this work), then plant new grass seed.

Other weed grasses. Many grasses that are too coarse or the wrong color for lawns can be hand-pulled easily. Most of these grasses have dense roots that leave a hole when removed. Dig a little peat moss into the bare patch to bring it up to lawn level, then reseed.

If an unknown lawn weed continues to grow despite removal or chemical treatment, pull up a sampling of the weed and take it to a nurseryman or county agricultural advisor for identification and advice.

Leafy weeds. For spot treatment of leafy weeds use weed oil, but handle it carefully because it will kill any other plant it touches. Applicator sticks containing weedicide can also be used for spot treatment.

Chemical control of leafy weeds consists of spraying on a phenoxy compound that resembles a plant growth hormone. This material is absorbed by the weed, making it grow so fast that it dies. The compound is sold as 2,4-D or 2,4,5-TP. You'll find 2,4,5-TP more effective for certain weeds such as oxalis or chickweed; check the label for specific directions on how to apply. (Both chemicals will be more effective if you feed and water the lawn first.)

Handle hormone sprays with as much caution as you would insect poisons. Choose a still day for spraying; hormone sprays carried away by a breeze may disfigure or kill other broad-leafed garden plants. Set the sprayer for a dense spray. Avoid hitting your skin and clothing and wash thoroughly after spraying. (*Caution:* Never use a sprayer that has held chemical hormone sprays for general garden spraying.)

Some lawn fertilizers contain additives for leafy weed control. These fertilizers may be a partial or a complete solution. Read the labels and follow the directions carefully.

Lawn fertilizers-and how to use them

Feeding a lawn ought to be a simple matter of common sense—when growth slows down and the deep green color fades to a yellowish shade, it's time to apply a nitrogen fertilizer. Actually this approach is complicated by the wide range of fertilizers available, and the diversified methods in treatment and application.

CHECK LABELS FOR NITROGEN CONTENT

The nitrogen that grass needs for growth can come from various organic or inorganic sources. You may find it listed under the following names:

Nitrate or nitrogenous—nitrogen in an immediately available form, regardless of air and soil temperature.

Ammoniacal or ammonic—bacteria is needed to break down the ammonia into nitrates.

Organic—bacteria is needed to work on sludge, cottonseed meal, or other products that come from plants or animals to form nitrates. These products work slowly.

Urea—a compound that is more complex than ammonia; bacteria convert it to ammonia, then to nitrates.

Urea-form, urea-formaldehyde, or "slow release"—artificially compounded to give slow, long-term release of usable nitrates.

UNDERSTANDING FORMULA NUMBERS

Whatever the product, the package label should have three numbers such as 6-4-2. The first number is the percentage of nitrogen, the second phosphorus, and the

third potassium (for information on converting numbers to actual pounds, see page 5). If one of the numbers is zero, then that element isn't included. The University of California Agricultural Extension recommends applying 1 pound of actual nitrogen per 1,000 square feet once a month. If you buy a fertilizer with the elements listed as 6-4-2, you will need to apply it at the rate of 16 pounds per 1,000 square feet each month.

WATERING-IN IS IMPORTANT

Most package labels state that the fertilizer must be watered in thoroughly after application. Do this without fail. If you leave any dry particles on the grass or you just dampen the grass slightly, you may end up with burned spots or even areas where the grass was killed.

ADDING IRON IN DRY CLIMATES

In regions with little rainfall, lawns may yellow despite your care. This condition is often caused from chlorosis (iron deficiency). To correct it, apply either iron chelate or iron sulfate. For iron chelate, follow package directions. For iron sulfate, spread 5 pounds per 1,000 square feet (handle with care because it stains paving).

HOW TO APPLY FERTILIZERS

On these pages, three of the most popular fertilizer spreading methods are illustrated. Whichever you choose to use, be sure to use the right amount of fertilizer and spread it evenly.

Also be sure to clean up your applicators thoroughly after use, particularly the wheeled hopper. Don't wash off a metal hopper unless you plan to dry and oil it; just spin the wheel and tap the side.

By hand. This method can be used for any product, but it's the safest with organic fertilizers since they don't burn grass as easily as chemical fertilizers. Go one way across the entire lawn (see photograph at left), applying the fertilizer at full strength, then repeat at right angles applying only half as much. If you think you've applied too much fertilizer in certain areas, rake lightly to scatter the material.

Liquid feeding. A hose end proportioner is far better than a watering can, but work fast. Divide the lawn in half with sticks or rope and work evenly, trying to reach the middle when the proportioner is half full, then finish as it empties.

Hopper spreader. Wheeled hoppers really only work properly if you own them and care for them. They must be kept clean and in good condition. Look over the illustrations of spreading patterns on the next page. You'll use the open-and-shut lever often. You spread a strip of fertilizer, close the opening, and reposition the hopper for the next strip, putting it into motion before you open the lever.

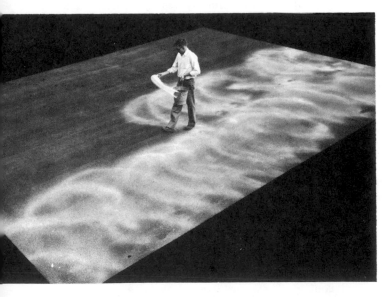

Handcast fertilizer *by walking slowly, casting parallel strips, then crossing at right angles for even coverage.*

Liquid feeding

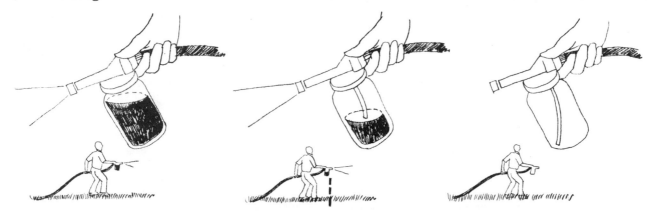

Fill proportioner with correct amount of fertilizer and water. Mark halfway point on lawn and on proportioner. Walking evenly, start spraying.

Halfway point should be reached when proportioner is half empty. If remaining amount is more or less than half, you are not spraying evenly.

Continue along second half of lawn, reaching end as bottle empties. Move proportioner up and down to spread spray evenly over the surface.

Hopper feeding

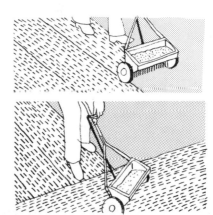

Two strips at each end of lawn give you turning room with hopper spreader. You want an even pattern with no overlaps or uncovered strips. To get this even effect, shut off hopper just as you reach end strips, then turn and start moving forward before you reopen hopper at edge of cross strip.

Hopper wheel must roll just inside previous fertilizer strip to avoid leaving gaps. Be sure to shut lever at the end, or you'll give a double dose.

Avoid these hopper mistakes

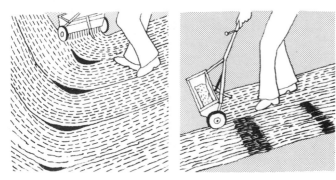

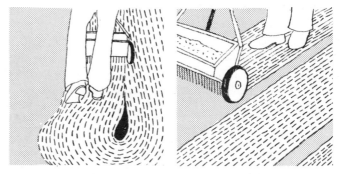

Using hopper like lawn mower will result in uncovered areas at every turn. They will show up later as yellow or pale marks. Uneven walking or stopping and starting gives double dose, may burn grass in rectangular patches.

Hairpin turns leave teardrop-shaped areas which will become yellow or pale as fertilized grass turns green. Unless you set one hopper wheel just inside previous track, a strip the full length of lawn will not be fertilized.

Ground covers

Ground covers usually require far less maintenance, feeding, and watering than lawn grasses. Wherever you want a uniform carpet of green but don't want to cope with the difficulties of keeping a lawn healthy, consider ground covers. However, keep in mind that ground covers should not be used in heavy traffic areas.

Ground covers are sold in various forms. For example, junipers may come in gallon-sized metal or plastic containers, whereas ice plant may be in a flat or small plastic container.

The chart on these two pages lists a number of popular ground covers. Your nursery may stock other varieties that will do as well. Before you make a final choice, consider these points: How much cold will that plant take? How fast will it grow? Does it need sun or shade? How far apart should the plants be spaced?

To plant a ground cover, prepare the soil as described on pages 56–57. (For some plants, it is not necessary to level and roll the ground, but ground hugging plants like ajuga or thyme require a smooth planting surface.)

You can grow some ground covers from plant divisions or cuttings. Examples of easily divided plants are ajuga, duchesnea, and thyme (*T. serpyllum*). Cuttings from ivy (*Hedera*), honeysuckle (*Lonicera*), and the vincas will root easily. To root them, use any one of the methods described on pages 40 and 41.

NAME OF PLANT	Hardy to	Where common: entire country (US); Rockies and eastward (E); California-Arizona (CA); Pacific Northwest (NW)	How fast to cover ground	Steep slopes (over 25%)	Large areas (over 500 sq. ft.)	Small areas (under 500 sq. ft.)	Full sun	Sun to medium shade	Medium shade to full shade	Tolerates dry or poor soil	Tolerates acid, moist soil
Achillea tomentosa	Sub-zero	US	Rapid			●	●	●		●	
Aegopodium podograria	Sub-zero	E	Rapid	●	●	●	●	●	●	●	●
Ajuga reptans	3°	US	Rapid	●	●	●	●	●			
Anthemis nobilis	0°	US	Mod.	●	●	●	●	●		●	
Arctostaphylos uva-ursi	Sub-zero	US	Slow	●	●	●	●	●		●	●
Asarum caudatum	Sub-zero	US	Mod.		●	●			●		●
Baccharis pilularis	3°	CA	Rapid	●	●		●	●		●	
Bergenia crassifolia	15°	US	Mod.		●	●		●	●		●
Cerastium tomentosum	Sub-zero	US	Rapid	●	●	●	●	●		●	
Ceratostigma plumbaginoides	Sub-zero	US	Mod. to rapid	●	●	●	●	●		●	
Cornus canadensis	Sub-zero	E, NW	Slow to mod.			●	●	●			●
Cotoneaster adpressa	Sub-zero	US	Slow to mod.	●	●	●	●	●		●	
C. dammeri	Sub-zero	US	Slow to mod.	●	●	●	●	●		●	
C. horizontalis	Sub-zero	US	Mod.	●	●	●	●	●		●	
C. microphylla	5°	US	Mod.	●	●	●	●	●		●	
Dianthus	Sub-zero	US	Mod.			●	●			●	
Duchesnea indica	Sub-zero	US	Rapid		●		●	●	●		●

NAME OF PLANT	Hardy to	Where common: entire country (US); Rockies and eastward (E); California-Arizona (CA); Pacific Northwest (NW)	How fast to cover ground	Steep slopes (over 25%)	Large areas (over 500 sq. ft.)	Small areas (under 500 sq. ft.)	Full sun	Sun to medium shade	Medium shade to full shade	Tolerates dry or poor soil	Tolerates acid, moist soil
Euonymus fortunei	Sub-zero	US	Slow to mod.	●	●	●	●	●	●		●
E.f. 'Colorata'	Sub-zero	US	Slow to mod.		●	●	●	●	●		●
E.f. radicans	Sub-zero	US	Mod.	●	●	●	●	●	●		●
E.f. 'Vegeta'	Sub-zero	US	Slow to mod.	●	●	●	●	●	●		●
Fragaria chiloensis	0°	CA, NW	Rapid	●	●	●	●	●			●
Gazania	10°	CA	Rapid	●	●	●	●			●	
Hedera helix	Sub-zero	US	Rapid	●	●	●	●	●	●		●
Hypericum calycinum	0°	US	Rapid	●	●		●	●	●		
Ice plant	15 to 25°	CA	Rapid	●	●	●	●				
Juniperus chinensis 'Pfitzer Compacta'	Sub-zero	US	Mod.	●	●		●			●	
J. conferta	Sub-zero	US	Mod.	●	●	●	●				●
Liriope muscari	Sub-zero	US	Mod.			●			●		
Lonicera japonica 'Halliana'	Sub-zero	US	Rapid	●	●		●	●		●	●
Nepeta hederacea	Sub-zero	US	Rapid		●		●	●	●		●
Pachistima canbyi	Sub-zero	E, NW	Slow to mod.		●	●	●	●			●
Pachysandra terminalis	Sub-zero	US	Rapid		●	●			●		●
Phlox subulata	Sub-zero	US	Rapid	●	●	●	●	●			●
Phyla nodiflora	0°	CA, NW	Rapid	●	●		●			●	
Polygonum capitatum	20°	CA	Mod. to rapid			●	●	●			●
Roses — 'Mermaid'	0°	US	Rapid	●	●		●				
Rosmarinus officinalis 'Lockwood de Forest'	3°	CA, NW	Slow at first	●	●	●	●			●	
Santolina chamaecyparissus	0°	US	Rapid	●	●	●	●			●	
Sarcococca humilis	Sub-zero	US	Slow			●			●		●
Sedum	0 to 15°	US	Rapid	●	●	●	●	●		●	
Thymus lanuginosus	Sub-zero	US	Rapid		●	●	●	●		●	
T. serpyllum	Sub-zero	US	Rapid		●	●	●	●		●	
Vinca major	0°	CA, NW	Rapid	●	●			●	●		●
Vinca minor	Sub-zero	US	Rapid	●	●	●		●	●		●

CONTAINER GARDENING
...having your plants where you want them

Have you ever wished you could bring a luxurious blooming azalea into your living room, or enjoy the fragrance of a blooming Meyer lemon when the temperature outside is still below freezing? You can turn these wishes into daily enjoyment if the plants are grown in handsome containers that can be moved wherever you like.

Whether you choose to bring a plant indoors or simply give it a prominent place on the patio or deck, container gardening allows you to move a plant when you want to, regardless of the season or transplanting conditions. And because you can create the proper soil condition (see directions below) and protect a plant from extreme temperatures, you can grow it wherever you like.

CAREFUL WATERING AND FEEDING ARE ESSENTIAL

Plants in containers require more attention to watering and soil condition than plants in the ground. You should water a container plant whenever the top inch or so of soil feels dry (in hot weather, some containers may require watering twice a day). Be sure to water enough so that the water begins to run out of the drainage holes. And if you're planning to be away from home for a few days, tightly group your container plants in a sheltered area; the plants will protect each other from the heat, cutting down moisture loss.

Unless the water in your area has a very low mineral content, salts will build up in containers, occasionally burning leaves or even killing some plants. To prevent this from happening, periodically flush out the soil by allowing water to trickle slowly into the container until it is saturated; or fill the pot several times in succession, allowing it to drain thoroughly. If leaf edges still show signs of burning (the edges turn brown and become brittle), submerge the pot in a tub filled with water (see illustration on page 23).

The frequent watering which is necessary to maintain container plants, unfortunately flushes away any added fertilizer. The best way to keep a plant fertilized is to feed it every week using one fourth the recommended strength.

TRANSPLANTING TECHNIQUES

Because feeder roots of container plants tend to mass next to the container wall, most plants should be transplanted to slightly larger pots from time to time or they will become pot bound and stop growing. Choose a new container that allows for two or three inches of new soil around the root ball. Guard against putting your plant into a much larger container—the unused soil may become soggy and sour and kill the plant before it has time to send out enough root growth. A day before transplanting, water the plant well. Then, remove the plant from its container, lightly scrape the root ball to stimulate the feeder roots, and set it in the larger pot on a bed

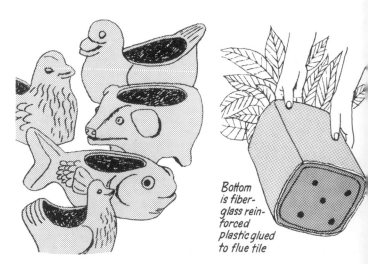

Bottom is fiberglass reinforced plastic glued to flue tile

Barrels *cut in half make attractive oversized containers. Some nurseries may sell them pre-cut and ready for use.*

Novelty containers *on left are made with terra cotta. You can make square flue tiles with fiberglass bottoms glued on.*

of new soil mix (see below). Then gradually add soil until the pot is filled, tamping the surface gently to avoid air pockets.

WHICH POTTING MIX?

A good planting mix is probably the most important element in container gardening. If you want to make up your own potting mix, use the ingredients listed for one of the three different mixes in the chart below. The basic mix is good for growing most plants; the exceptions are acid-loving plants which require the acid mix. The lightweight mix is best used for house plants or for container plants that require frequent moving.

Guard against substituting a *raw* wood product for one of the ingredients because it will quickly use up any fertilizer you add, leaving the plant without the proper nourishment.

The amount of ingredients listed for a small quantity of basic mix will fill about 18 pots, 12 inches in diameter. The larger quantity of basic mix will give you a cubic yard. Whether you make the small or large quantity,

BASIC MIX (For a Large Quantity)

(Suitable for all but ericaceous plants such as azalea, heather, rhododendron.)

2/3 yard	nitrogen stabilized bark, redwood sawdust, or other organic matter
1/3 yard	sandy loam or uniform fine sand
6 pounds	0-10-10 or equivalent dry fertilizer
10 pounds	dolomite limestone

BASIC MIX (For a Small Quantity)

16 gallons	nitrogen stabilized bark, redwood sawdust, or other organic matter
8 gallons	sandy loam or uniform fine sand
1-1/3 cups	0-10-10 or equivalent dry fertilizer
1-3/4 cups	dolomite limestone

LIGHTWEIGHT MIX

(Ideal for indoor planters or outside container plants in sheltered areas. This mix may not provide sufficient support for taller plants in windy situations.)

2 parts	basic mix (above)
1 part	perlite

ACID MIX

(For azalea, heather, rhododendron, etc.)

4 or 5 parts	coarse-textured peat moss
1 part	composted oak leaf mold

the basic mix will require additional frequent feedings of nitrogen, since it will not retain fertilizer very well (use a quarter-strength fertilizer weekly).

If you prefer to use your own formula for making a soil mix, make sure it doesn't include dense clay. Clay soil retains water, often drowning container plants.

Before putting plants in containers, make sure the mix is damp but not wet (if you're using new clay pots, soak them before planting so they will not rob moisture from the soil mix). Cover the container drain hole with small pieces of broken clay pots. Then check the consistency of the mix—it must be the same throughout the container to allow capillary action to draw water down to the roots. Fill the pot with soil mix to within ½ inch of the top. Water slowly to give the mix a chance to settle, adding more if needed.

Prepare soil mix *by putting ingredients into large pile, tossing them into a second pile to mix, and then tossing again if the mix is not blended the first time.*

Scatter fertilizer *and limestone over the blended organic matter and loam or sand. If you want a lightweight mix, use this stage to spread perlite over basic ingredients.*

Toss again *once or twice to blend in fertilizer (and perlite if you are using it). If you are only making a small quantity of soil mix, use your hands as mixing tools.*

Easy-to-make wooden containers

The 11 planters shown on these two pages have one thing in common: They were handmade using scrap lumber. To make some of these planters requires a little more carpentry skill than the others, but none of them are really difficult to build.

Before deciding which one suits your needs, consider these points: 1) Large containers should come apart easily so you can trim roots or transplant. 2) If you want to move heavy containers from place to place, construct a small wooden platform on wheels. 3) Containers on wooden decks or patios should sit on blocks of wood, tiles, or bricks for better drainage and so that the deck or patio surface will dry quickly after each watering.

Sloping sides *of planter support overlapping juniper branches, accent the shape of plant (hebe) at center.*

Weathered wood *was used to make this wall-hung planter. Texture blends into garden setting, shows off plant foliage.*

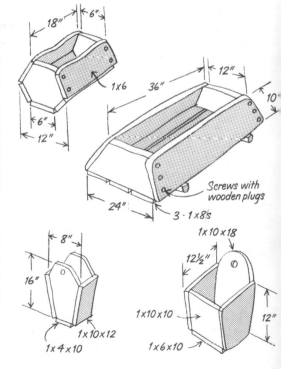

Hexagonal planter *(above) is easy to build. Draw pattern for hexagon-shaped ends on heavy construction paper. Follow the pattern in cutting scrap lumber. Join the two ends with planks and drill holes if you want to hang planter. Hanging feedbag planter (at right) has little space for root growth, so use it for strawberry plants or succulents that can grow with roots crowded in narrow space. The sketches at far right will guide you in cutting and joining lumber for planters shown on this page.*

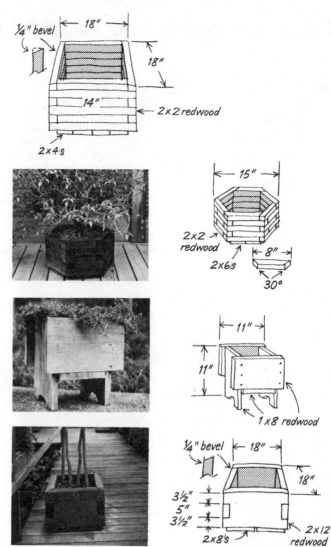

Nails and glue were used to join redwood 2 by 2 s for sides of this planter. Exposed ends make interesting pattern. Bottom is 2 by 4 redwood with narrow drainage spaces.

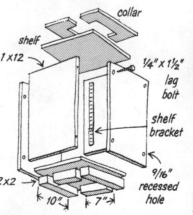

Disguising container inside, this box can hold 5-gallon nursery cans or other pots for temporary plant display. Bring in a lemon or azalea growing in a nursery can and set it in this type of display box for a special event, then return it to the garden. Similar boxes can be used for dramatic display of house plants like asparagus fern or Boston fern. For construction details, see sketch above. Collar is used to hide unappealing containers, but can be left out for house plant displays if you wish.

Gardening in hanging baskets

Plants that sprawl and scramble when planted in the ground take on a new dimension when you plant them in hanging containers. Nurseries stock hanging pots and baskets already planted and ready to hang. You can also buy the empty container and plant your own basket. Use wire baskets lined with sphagnum moss, or ceramic, plastic, or wooden containers designed for hanging. For a ball-of-flowers effect, use a moss-lined wire basket, placing the plants in the sides, bottom, and top. For information on soil mixes and watering techniques, see pages 23 and 65.

The list below suggests good foliage plants suitable for hanging containers; the chart on the opposite page lists flowering plants. Besides these plants, many of the aromatic herbs and small-fruited peppers and tomatoes do well in hanging baskets.

Bar Harbor juniper (*J. horizontalis* 'Bar Harbor'). Long, trailing, ground-hugging; steel blue foliage turns purplish in fall. New growth bright green. Sun.

Bearberry cotoneaster (*C. dammeri*). Creeping prostrate stems follow contours of the container, hang far below. Bright red fruits in fall.

Blue carpet juniper (*J. h.* 'Wiltonii'). Flattest juniper; silver blue needles. Sun.

Boston fern (*Nephrolepis exaltata* 'Bostoniense'). Long fronds droop to 3 feet below container in open shade. Direct sun may burn the plant.

Grape ivy (*Cissus rhombifolia*). Familiar house plant in colder areas; elegant outdoor hanging container plant where mild. Shade or partial shade; takes sun in cool, moist climates.

Ivy (*Hedera*). Small and miniature-leafed forms make ideal hanging plants. All are more lush in full shade.

Mirror plant (*Coprosma repens*, often sold as *C. baueri*). Uncommonly handsome when trailing branches drape over the edge of a suspended container. Part shade; at its best in cool fog belt.

Plectranthus (*P. australis*). Leaves are thick and succulent, with scalloped edges. Insignificant white or pale lavender flowers. Tender below 24°. Shade.

Shore juniper (*Juniperus conferta*). Bright green, soft needled. Sun or part shade.

Spider plant (*Chlorophytum comosum*). Evergreen perennial with curving leaves tipped with small duplicates of mother plant that are easy to remove and pot up. Partial shade, moisture.

Sprenger asparagus (*A. sprengeri*). Tough and easy, yet extremely graceful. Takes sun but more lush in shade.

Spider plant *is effectively displayed from hanging pot. Ends have room for growth, can fall where they like.*

Boston fern *is one of several ferns that do well in hanging pots. Provide shade, indirect light, high humidity.*

Shore juniper *forms dense ball above its clay pot. You can hang this plant in sun or part shade.*

Some high-wire favorites

THE PLANTS	The flowers	When they bloom	Where they grow	Additional facts and opinions
Abutilon megapotamicum	Profusion of drooping yellow flowers with red calyces—like Chinese lanterns.	Summer to fall; nearly all year in mildest climates.	Part shade or sun. Can take light frosts.	Cut back arching sprays occasionally. Spray to control whitefly.
Begonia 'Richmondensis'	Drooping clusters of salmon pink from deeper-colored buds.	Spring to fall; nearly everblooming where winters are mild.	Part shade, but needs good light for heavy flowering.	Excellent foliage and plant habit. Cut back near soil level when new growth begins in spring.
Begonia semperflorens BEDDING OR WAX BEGONIA	White, pink, or red; single or double.	Late spring to fall, or nearly everblooming.	Part shade; needs ample light for bloom.	Double pink and double red best for baskets. Leaners, not trailers. Pinch to shape plants.
Begonia tuberhybrida TUBEROUS BEGONIA	White, pink, red, yellow, orange; bicolors and blends.	Summer and fall near coast; shorter season inland ends with onset of hot weather.	Part shade with good light. Inland, requires more shade, added humidity for success.	Be sure to buy trailing kind for hanging basket use.
Beloperone guttata SHRIMP PLANT	Shrimplike clusters of coppery or chartreuse bracts. True flowers white, inconspicuous.	Nearly all year, but suspends flowering in cold weather.	Bright light, but not hottest sun. 'Chartreuse' variety needs more shade. Takes light frost.	Cut back in late winter. Pinch and prune to establish form, make plants compact.
Calceolaria integrifolia	Clusters of pouch-shaped, yellow to brown-red flowers.	Summer and fall; late spring in warmest southern regions.	Bright light, but not hot sun. Can take considerable frost.	Bright yellow 'Golden Nugget' best known. Prune back in late winter.
Campanula isophylla ITALIAN BELLFLOWER, STAR OF BETHLEHEM	Profusion of white or light blue, bell-shaped, starry-pointed flowers.	Late summer and fall.	Part shade with good light. Roots fairly hardy. Tops die back after flowering.	Blue one has gray, fuzzy leaves; white one has smooth, green leaves. Cut back tops after bloom.
Felicia amelloides (Agathea coelestis) BLUE MARGUERITE	Blue, daisylike, with yellow centers.	Almost all year.	Sun or light shade. Can take moderate frost.	Needs sun to set buds; budded plants bloom well in shade. Needs grooming, shaping; cutting back in winter.
Fuchsia hybrida FUCHSIA	Drooping, white, pink, red, orange, lavender, purple; bicolors common.	Summer and fall; nearly all year in mildest coastal gardens.	Partial shade with good light. Mature wood fairly hardy.	Hundreds of good trailing kinds, with new introductions every year. Responds quickly to feeding and shaping.
Impatiens walleriana BUSY LIZZIE	Flat, 1 to 2-inch flowers in white, pink, orange, red, lavender, violet.	Spring to fall in cooler climates; nearly all year in mildest areas.	Part shade with good light. Tender; usually grown as an annual.	Brilliant and dependable. Double forms (scarce) set no seed, won't scatter seedlings on ground underneath.
Lantana montevidensis (L. sellowiana)	Clustered lilac-lavender flowers.	Spring to frost.	Sun. Takes moderate frost, average soil.	Needs sun and warmth to bloom. Prune back hard when plants get bare at base.
Lobelia erinus	Profuse show of small blue or white flowers.	Summer and fall; longest bloom where summers are fairly cool.	Partial shade; full sun near coast. Grown as an annual.	Variety 'Sapphire' is best trailer; flowers deep blue with white eye.
Lotus berthelotii	Scarlet, beak-shaped flowers contrast nicely with gray foliage.	Summer.	Sun. Perennial, but tender to frost.	Needs heat and excellent drainage. Cut plants back when bare at base. Short bloom season.
Pelargonium domesticum LADY WASHINGTON PELARGONIUM	Clustered flowers in white, pink, lavender, coral, red, often with contrasting blotch.	Spring and early summer; longest summer season where summers are cool.	Partial shade with good light; full sun in fog belt. Tender to sharp frosts.	Select weak stemmed varieties that will lean or trail. Prune back in September or October, *not* spring.
Pelargonium peltatum IVY GERANIUM	White, pink, lavender, red clusters; single or double.	All summer and fall.	Full sun; partial shade in hot summer areas. Tender to sharp frosts.	Natural trailers that take heat well. Bushier growth with pinching.
Petunia hybrida PETUNIA	White, pink, lavender, blue, red, purple, creamy yellow, bicolored; single or double.	Spring, summer, fall. Winter, spring in southwest desert.	Sun or light shade. Hardy; usually grown as annuals.	Among easiest and showiest of basket plants. Many excellent kinds available. Outstanding singles: Cascade strain.
Tropaeolum majus NASTURTIUM	Creamy white and yellow to pink and red; single or double.	Spring, summer.	Sun or light shade. Grown as annuals.	Easy and colorful; rather short bloom season.

Raised beds and retaining walls

Whether raised beds and/or retaining walls are for you depends, to a large extent, on the way your property was graded. Perhaps your garden soil was swept away when the building site was graded, leaving only rock or hardpan. Raised beds are a good answer. Or, grading may have left only a short, steep slope for gardening. A retaining wall is a likely solution.

For centuries Asians have grown rice successfully on mountain slopes by forming rock terraces to keep the soil from washing away and to retain water. Water-holding, however, is likely to be a problem for you rather than a benefit. In a wet season, a retaining wall that holds back water may give way, spilling your garden into the house. The raised beds and retaining walls shown on these two pages have good water drainage.

If you should choose to use a solid material (such as masonry or concrete) to hold back a hillside, then it must have numerous "weep" holes or a system of tile drains that carry water away. Weep holes let water pour out in front of the wall; drains, although expensive and complicated, are better where you want to direct water away to the side.

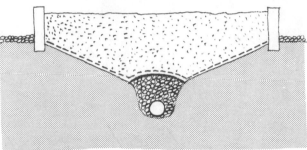

Low planting beds are dug out as shown in sketch above to provide room for root growth, then filled with a good soil mixture. At the bottom of each hole, a wide trench holds drain tile and crushed rock covered with tar paper. Drains are joined underground, lead to downslope so excess water can flow away. Drain system is needed only where native soil is impermeable (see page 14).

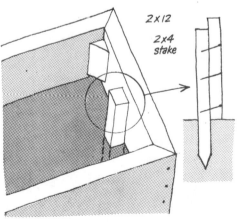

2 x 12

2 x 4 stake

Redwood boxes, built of 2 by 12 lumber, hold vegetables and cutting flowers in small garden. Boxes have no bottoms so roots grow into soil. Gravel 1 inch thick between boxes keeps weeds down, forms walkways. Treat stakes that keep sides in place with copper solution to prevent rot.

Changing driveway grade or other construction grading may leave soil banks that crumble easily, baring the roots of existing trees or shrubs. This broken concrete wall holds earth, allows drainage.

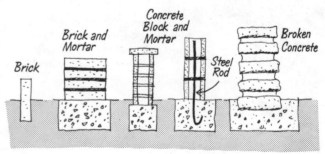

Low masonry walls can be built by an amateur. The sketch above shows construction details for several kinds of material. Note underground concrete footing used for each material. The concrete should be poured in a square trench that is slightly wider than the wall itself. Steel reinforcement for hollow concrete block must be set into footing at the start. Don't try to build masonry walls more than a foot high because they may crack or tilt as they settle. Also, high walls require provisions for drainage.

INDOOR GARDENING
...plants for any room in the house

House plants have come a long way since the days when wealthy Victorians grew ferns in their conservatories and only those who could afford it had potted palms gracing their homes. Nowadays house plants of all sizes, shapes, and varieties are displayed in the living room, the kitchen, the bathroom—anywhere there's space.

If you've never grown house plants before or if you have tried but with little success, it is important to know that finding a good location for your house plant is the most crucial part of its care.

Most plants dislike dry heat. If you are accustomed to keeping the thermostat turned up high, choose a variety that thrives in moist heat and keep it in the kitchen or bathroom.

Some points to consider: A few plants will survive in a dark hall—both sentry palms and aspidistra have been known to do so—but most plants will die without adequate light. Indirect or north light is best for most indoor plants. (*Caution:* Never set any plant in a south or west window; hot sun coming through these exposures can quickly bake or burn tender plants.) Because a plant will lean toward the most dependable source of light, many gardeners suggest giving the container a quarter turn each week.

If your plant isn't doing well in one location, try moving it to another spot. But if it is doing well don't experiment with moving it around.

Feeding your plants. All house plants should be regularly fertilized with any one of the numerous products offered by florists and nurseries including tablets, powders you mix with water, liquids, or fish fertilizer. Guard against overfeeding; follow label directions carefully.

Aspidistra

Dark green glossy leaves to 2½ feet long, 4 inches wide. Prefers good light, will grow in dark corners. Tolerates some neglect.

Avocado

Dark green leaves. Can grow tall. Start from seed in water or moist soil. Sprouts slowly; seedlings need good light, lots of water.

Begonia

Many kinds with foliage varied by size, shape, color. Give indirect light; keep soil moist. Root cuttings in water.

Bird's nest fern

Apple green, undivided fronds to 4 feet long, 8 inches wide, unfurl from center of plant. Give good indirect light, lots of water.

Boston fern

Drooping fronds effectively displayed in hanging container or in pot on a stand. Give north light; keep soil moist; mist often.

Chamaedorea palm

Grows slowly to 3 or 4 feet tall. Tolerates poor light, crowded roots, infrequent watering. You can plant several in one container.

Coleus

Leaf colors in shades of yellow, orange, red, magenta, green. Give strong light, lots of water. Cuttings root well.

Columnea crassifolia

Trailing plant with striking orange flowers. Give it high humidity, good light, ample water. Soil must drain well.

Columnea 'Stavanger'

Trailing, small-leafed plant with large red-orange flowers. Requires high humidity, good light, ample water.

Croton

Grows to 15 inches with big leathery leaves marked in bright colors. Give it high humidity, good light, lots of water.

Crown of thorns

Thorny stems to 4 feet. Has red flower bracts. Likes indirect light, average water. Can tolerate a little drought.

Dieffenbachia

Enormous green and white leaves on a sturdy cane. Tolerates low light; needs average watering. If it gets stalky, cut off top and replant.

Dizygotheca

Dark green 4 to 9-inch-long leaflets in fanlike clusters. Will grow large if soil is kept moist. Likes indirect light.

Ficus benjamina

Mass of shiny, delicate leaves, 2 to 5 inches long. Needs bright indirect light, average amounts of water.

Fiddleleaf fig

Leaves to 15 inches long, 10 inches wide grow from main stem. Can withstand low light. Wipe leaves clean with water.

Fluffy ruffles fern

Variety of Boston fern with dark green, upright fronds that give a lacy effect. Requires north light, moist soil.

Grape ivy

Bronzy, dark green leaves often in groups of three. Climbs by tendrils. Tolerates low light; needs average water.

Myers asparagus fern

Erect plumelike branches are shaped like foxtails. Likes average light, water. If leaves turn yellow, increase light level.

(Continued on next page)

Philodendron

Many varieties, from vines with 5-inch leaves to erect plants with 3-foot leaves. Likes humidity. Let soil dry out between waterings.

Piggy-back plant

Fuzzy, heart-shaped leaves; tiny plants grow from V of the heart. Needs good light, moist soil, good air circulation.

Pregnant onion

Bulb produces strap-shaped leaves 2 feet long. May have greenish flowers in spring. Likes sun, average water.

Pteris cretica

Attractive fern with oddly shaped fronds to 18 inches. Give medium light. Requires cool temperatures and lots of water.

Sansevieria

Long, variegated straplike leaves stand straight up. Tolerates a wide range of conditions. Be careful not to overwater.

Schefflera

Big leaves with 7 to 16 leaflets in a fan shape on long stems. Container must be large enough for root growth. Needs average water, light.

Sentry palm

Large, long-stemmed fronds spray out of trunk like a fountain. Tolerates low light and occasional lack of water.

Spider plant

Green and white, grasslike leaves. Stems support new plants at stem end. Does well in hanging pots. Needs lots of light, average water.

Splitleaf philodendron

Not a true philodendron. If it grows too tall, air layer the top at leaf node and repot (see page 77). Likes good light, average water.

Sprenger asparagus

Trailing version of Myers asparagus. Produces white, scented flowers, red fruit. Needs good light. Can tolerate drought.

Ti plant

Variegated leaves to 12 inches in colors from red to yellow. Plants grow wide and tall. Requires good light and ample water.

Wandering Jew

Trailing plant with leaves from dark green to pink and white. Cuttings root easily in water. Needs average light, watering.

Watering house plants

How much water do indoor plants need? Unfortunately there is no simple formula to follow. Each plant has its individual watering needs. The longer you tend your house plants the more aware you'll become of the actual amount of water each one requires. One way to check a plant's moisture level is to feel the soil. When the top inch or so feels dry, it's time to add water. Keep in mind that a soggy plant will die sooner than a dry one.

One of the best ways to water a house plant is to submerge it in water to just over the container rim; leave it there at least until the air bubbles stop rising. An hour-long soak won't hurt it. Because most plants build up salts in the soil due to light watering and feeding, a long soaking helps flush some of the salts away.

If your water is very hard or is artificially softened, don't use it on your house plants. Instead, use bottled distilled water, or when you can, put out a container to catch rainwater.

It's always a good idea to rinse off the leaves of your plants while they're soaking. You can spray the foliage with a spray attachment at the sink, take the plant outdoors and wash it off with a fine spray from your garden hose, or gently clean each leaf with a soft damp cloth.

If you are going to be away for more than a week, you might want to consider using an automatic watering device. Several are available at nurseries or florist shops. Another way to keep your plants moist while you're away is to soak them thoroughly, drain them, then wrap the container and soil surface in a plastic bag or plastic kitchen wrap. It will keep the soil moist for quite a while, depending on the season of the year and the house temperature.

Metal-lined indoor planter *holds house plants. A little water in bottom humidifies the air around the leaves.*

Place small pots *in a plastic tub filled with water. Larger plants can be placed in laundry sink or bathtub.*

Rinse leaves *to remove dust, pests, increase humidity; or, as you can, set them out in a gentle rain.*

Gardening in a bottle or bowl

If you'd like to grow a few house plants, but the average temperature in your house is too high and the humidity level too low to grow most varieties, try planting moisture-loving varieties inside a bottle or bowl. The soil mix should be damp when you plant, so the plants can quickly create their own humid environment. *Caution: Be especially careful not to overwater these undrained containers.*

The right container for the right plant is the first consideration. Moisture-loving plants do better in bottles or closed containers because the air inside is very humid. Clear glass containers are best since they allow more light to reach the plants. Bottles of all sizes and prices are available at plant stores, homeware and glass shops, chemical supply houses, and even junk shops.

Before you plant, wash the container and allow it to dry completely. Then spread an inch of moistened, packaged, house plant soil mix inside—use a tube of rolled waxed paper as a funnel if the opening is small. Then add a thin layer of charcoal (available at nurseries or aquarium stores) over the first layer, and cover with more soil mix. Using a long stick, shape the planting surface and dig the first planting hole. Remove the soil from the roots of the plant and insert it into the planting hole (the gripper tool shown below is helpful). Cover the plant's roots. Then, plant the rest of the garden in the same manner.

For more information on planting in bottles and bowls, see the Sunset book, *Terrariums and Miniature Gardens.*

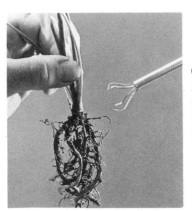

Claw gadget *helps in planting and removing plants, or even in arranging such decorations as pebbles or bits of weathered wood.*

Place plants *in a layer of moist soil and charcoal. Other containers you can use are aquariums, large brandy snifters, decorative jars, or porcelain bowls. Open containers require more attention to watering.*

Other handy tools: *Homemade bamboo pruner has razor blade inserted in split. Stick or bent wire can be used for digging. Short or long claw digging tools and other watering, misting devices are sold at nurseries, hardware stores.*

Multiplying house plants

A good many house plants can be propagated easily by taking leaf cuttings or by air layering. The photographs below show you how this can be done.

Leaf cuttings are best taken from plants with fleshy, long-stemmed leaves (Rex begonias and African violets).

Air layering is the method for propagating woody-stemmed plants such as a rubber plant or a fiddleleaf fig. With this method, the parent plant supports the air-layered section until it roots and can be cut off and planted.

Cut off leaf *of begonia or African violet. Trim the stem to 1 or 2 inches with a sharp knife or razor blade (be careful not to crush the stem when cutting).*

Place stem *in moist acid potting mix (see formula for making on page 65 or buy it ready made). Check for new growth by carefully lifting up the leaves.*

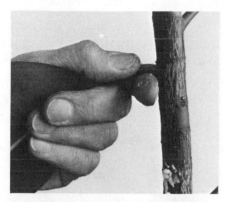 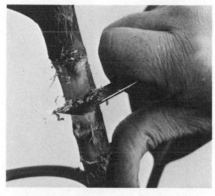 

Snap off a leaf *or two from the upper third portion of the main stem on rubber plants, other woody house plants.*

Scrape bark *from main stem with knife blade just below leaf you removed. New roots will grow where leaf was.*

Wrap scraped section *with handful of very moist sphagnum moss, covering edges of unscraped parts.*

Cover moss *with plastic, overlapping the ends and tying securely at top and bottom to keep moisture inside.*

New roots *will show through clear plastic wrap in about a month. Cut below roots to separate the new plant.*

Pot *the newly rooted portion. The parent plant will form a new branch or branches and continue to grow.*

STAKING, THINNING, PRUNING
... give your plants a helping hand

Most garden plants require some control over their size and shape in order to keep them attractive. Left to grow naturally, plants would quickly become straggly or rangy, often suffering serious damage from the elements. Illustrated below and on the opposite page are some of the everyday chores you can do to keep a plant tidy looking, control its growth, and improve its performance. (More specialized pruning techniques for roses and fruit trees and for the formal training of vines and espaliers are covered on pages 80–85.)

The materials you'll need are few: Plant stakes (ranging from thin lengths of green-painted bamboo to larger pieces of wood or metal) and some sort of tie (see photo at left below) that will keep plants growing in the desired direction.

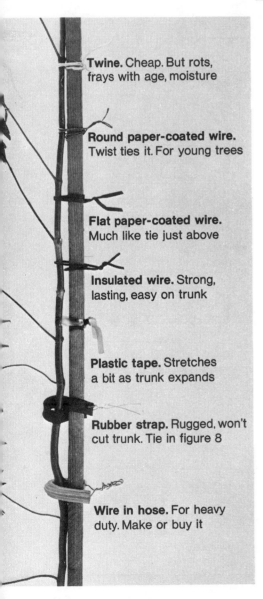

Twine. Cheap. But rots, frays with age, moisture

Round paper-coated wire. Twist ties it. For young trees

Flat paper-coated wire. Much like tie just above

Insulated wire. Strong, lasting, easy on trunk

Plastic tape. Stretches a bit as trunk expands

Rubber strap. Rugged, won't cut trunk. Tie in figure 8

Wire in hose. For heavy duty. Make or buy it

Plant ties *ranging from twine to hose and wire are sold at nurseries. Use top five ties for small plants.*

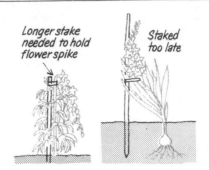

Stake flower spikes *of tall growers or they may snap off like delphinium at left, or bend like gladiolus at right.*

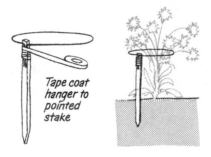

Tape coat hanger to pointed stake

Bend coat hanger *in a circle and tape to a stake to support a clump of plants or several long stems.*

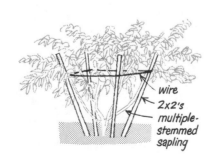

wire
2x2's
multiple-stemmed
sapling

Multiple trunks *of shrubs or small trees are tied to 2 by 2s with wire supporting the upper ends of the stakes.*

Use one stake *and figure-8 ties to support a number of plants. Either twine or wire ties work well.*

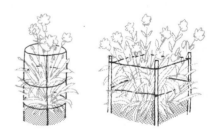

Make cylinder *of wire fencing or stretch twine around four stakes to keep tall growers upright.*

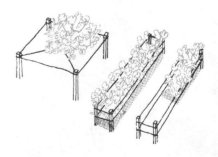

Wire-tied 2 by 2s *offer extra support for multiple-stemmed plants. Stakes and wire also work for cut flowers.*

Longer stake needed to hold flower spike

Staked too late

Pinching to direct shape. Whether you want a bushy plant with many branches or a plant with a tall stem or trunk and branches at the top, pinching off the growing tips of the plant accomplishes the goal. For bushy plants, use your thumb and finger to pinch off the tender growth tip of every branch. Dormant buds will then begin to grow somewhere along each branch that you pinched. For a taller stemmed plant, pinch off growth tips of all side branches. Let the main stem grow to the height you want, then pinch it to force branching.

Improving performance. Too many flower buds will produce small and crowded flowers. Too much fruit may break branches. To prevent this from happening, twist off some buds or green fruit here and there at any early stage.

Tidying up. Besides looking messy, dead leaves and flowers interfere with new growth and should be removed frequently. Heavily-flowering plants like marguerites or dwarf marigolds require very light shearing to keep them looking good.

Sucker removal. Botanically speaking, a sucker is a shoot that grows from a root or from an underground portion of a stem. Experienced gardeners would include shoots that grow from an understock below a bud or graft.

Wherever it sprouts, sucker growth can slow plant growth by diverting food and water to itself. If not removed, it can even kill the upper, more desirable part of the plant. To keep a plant free of suckers, rub off the tender buds as soon as they appear; clip off older shoots flush with the trunk.

Pinch back vertical of lavender plant (left) and leggy geranium (center) for bushiness. To produce tall trunked plant, remove side shoots (right), leave main bud.

Pinching buds and fruit produces better quality of both. Left, remove small camellia buds; center, remove smaller apricots. Right, pinch off old flower stalks to groom.

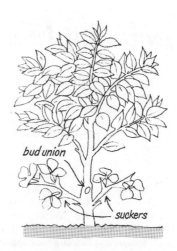

Thorny shoots of trifoliate orange often grow on grafted dwarf citrus. Note the different leaves on the short branches below the bud union. Remove branches like these flush with the trunk or they will take over and starve the upper, more desirable part of the plant.

Sucker branches on a grafted maple are not always obvious. First find the graft union along the trunk. It will be somewhat thicker than the rest of the stem. Cut any branches below the union flush with the trunk, then rub out any other suckers you find in the bud stage.

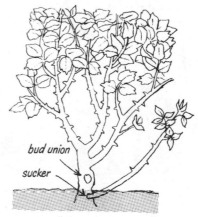

Rose suckers sometimes look very much like the top growth, but often are thornier or different in structure. If you can't tell, wait for a flower. Suckers never produce the same flowers as top growth. If sucker grows from underground, dig away soil to remove it at base.

Basic pruning techniques

In *nature* every plant eventually is pruned in some manner. It may be a simple matter of low branches on forest trees being shaded by higher ones until they wither and die and are removed in a sudden storm. Or it could be that tender new branches of small plants are accidentally knocked off by wild animals looking for food. In the long run, a plant growing naturally will take the shape that is best for its location and climate.

In a garden you can help things along by pruning. Your reason may be to get a better shape or size or more and bigger flowers and fruit. Whatever your intent, pruning should usually be done in such a way that the plant looks as if it were growing naturally. Espaliers, hedges, and topiary plants are some of the exceptions.

If the tip is removed, dormant buds all along the branch may begin to produce auxin. When you pinch off branch tips, as suggested on page 79, you signal the plant to produce new branches.

Pinching doesn't change the direction of plant growth —it just increases the number of stems and buds. To change the direction of a branch, you must find a fat bud growing in the direction you want the branch to grow. You then snip off the whole branch just above that bud. The bud will take over. For the same reason, you never pinch a branch that's vigorously growing faster than the rest of the plant (pinching only gives you several vigorous branches). Instead, you cut off the branch at the base, or at least to a bud located well below the rest of the foliage.

PINCHING PRODUCES NEW BUDS

Each branch tip of a plant produces a growth hormone called auxin. This hormone causes the tip bud to produce new tissue, drawing nourishment and water from the plant through the cambium layer just under the bark.

LEARN THE DIFFERENCES IN PLANT GROWTH

Before any major surgery, study a plant's growth habits. Each plant grows differently, and the right pruning tech-

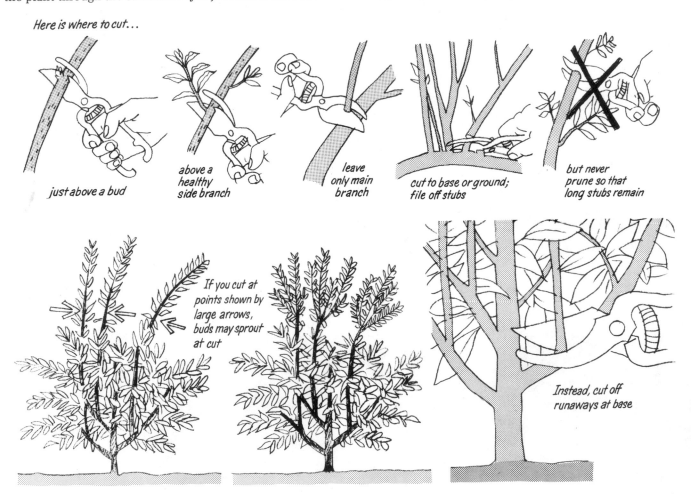

Here is where to cut...

just above a bud

above a healthy side branch

leave only main branch

cut to base or ground; file off stubs

but never prune so that long stubs remain

If you cut at points shown by large arrows, buds may sprout at cut

Instead, cut off runaways at base

Some branches of a shrub may grow much too long, spoiling the shape of the plant. If you cut them near top, bushy new growth will grow out below the cut, also spoiling the shape of the plant. Instead, cut as shown at far right.

Cut off runaway growth where it started to retain plant shape. Don't leave a stub when you cut.

niques for one plant may mean death or disfigurement for another. For example, privet will often sprout lush growth if you cut it back to bare twigs. Do the same pruning to a marguerite and you'll lose it. And, you'll find that the pruning of some plants will produce little new growth. A good example of this is the camellia—pinch it back and you may get only one replacement branch. To produce several branches, you must cut back to the point where last year's growth stopped and this year's began (look for a difference in bark color).

WHEN YOU'RE READY TO PRUNE

Some kind of pruning is necessary for most plants just before or at the beginning of the growing season. Major pruning on deciduous plants like fruit and roses is usually done in late winter when branches are bare. But you can also clean up, pinch back, or shear many plants in summer and fall—in fact, you have to if you want to keep a plant a certain size or shape.

The number one rule in pruning is: *Never make a cut at an arbitrary point along a branch.* Instead, cut just above a bud or a good branch, or make the cut flush with the trunk or base, trying to make the wound fairly small so bark will cover it quickly. If you cut between two buds leaving a stub, no nourishment will pass through the tissue below the cut. The stub above the bud will wither and die, offering a breeding ground for disease organisms that can damage the whole branch.

Shrubs and trees that produce flowers can be pruned after the flowers fade and just as new leaf growth is beginning. Since the plant is in an active growth stage, it will quickly heal the cuts you make. If you grow a plant specifically for cut flowers (roses perhaps) cut off every bloom with a view to shaping the plant; also, be sure to remove stubs and inferior branches.

Notch branch, *cut beyond notch, then cut stump.*

Seal cuts *to prevent disease, keep out rot.*

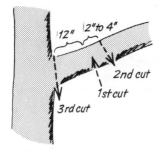

Cut back *frost bitten wood a little at a time.*

Use pole pruner *to trim high branches correctly.*

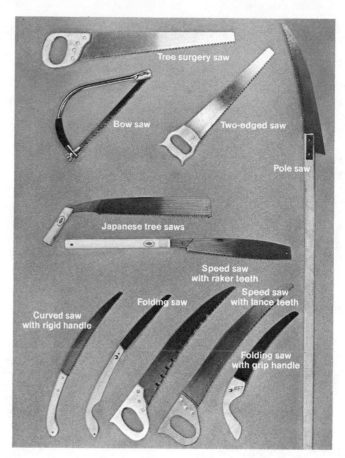

Pruning saws *come in a variety of sizes and shapes; saws may cut with pull stroke, push stroke, or both.*

Fruit trees and roses have specific pruning rules. Different kinds of fruit trees produce their crops in different ways, and roses come in so many forms that there is no single pruning rule. On the following pages you'll find illustrations that will help you deal with these particular plants.

TOOLS AND MATERIALS

Look over the different types of pruning saws on this page and the general pruning tools shown on page 95. The saw at the top of this page cuts as you push; it is a favorite of professional pruners who do heavy cutting. The two saws in the next row cut when you push and pull. All the other saws shown cut when you pull. The curved folding saw is best for a beginner. (Remember that all types should be wiped and oiled with care after use, since you're usually cutting wet green wood.)

Of the various cutting tools (excluding saws), you'll find a sturdy pair of pruning shears the handiest. They're light enough to carry with you whenever you go into the garden. You might also want to get the little specialty shears meant specifically for cutting flowers, but these are too small to serve as your only pruning tool. When your shears begin to crush or tear the plant tissue, it's time to have them sharpened.

Keep a can of tree sealing compound on hand to seal any big cuts you make—it helps keep out any disease organisms.

Pruning roses and fruit trees

Almost every garden has at least one representative of the family of plants that includes roses, cane berries, strawberries, apples, pears, cherries, quinces, peaches, nectarines, apricots, plums, and almonds. The woody members of this family require yearly pruning in order to produce the best flowers and fruit. How to go about this along with specific techniques are discussed below.

Roses. The illustrations below show you the right way to prune three different kinds of roses.

Although there are different schools of thought on rose pruning, here is one bit of advice to remember always: In addition to the major once-a-year pruning, prune a little all year long, cutting off spent flowers and trimming back branches that cross and tangle.

Fruit trees. Apple, pear, and cherry trees produce their fruit on little spurs that grow very slowly. They require only light pruning to remove inferior or damaged branches and twigs. (Prune trees are also slow growers, requiring the same kind of treatment.)

Peaches and nectarines are just the opposite. They grow vigorously, sending out long whips, and will get out of hand easily if you don't prune them severely. Keep in mind that last summer's new growth will give you this year's flowers and fruit. When you shorten and thin growth, always leave some of the previous year's new growth or the tree won't produce any fruit.

Apricots and plums grow fast like peaches and produce flowers and fruit on new wood. But they also produce fruit on slow-growing short spurs the way apples do. New branches that have grown too long or have become straggly can be completely removed without losing the whole fruit crop, but try to leave at least a piece of each new branch. By doing this, you'll increase your crop and the number of fruit spurs for the following years.

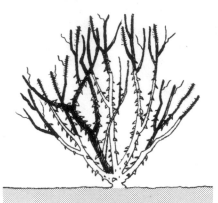

Dormant rose bush *on left can be pruned from January (mild climates) to early spring (cold climates). Cut out oldest canes, crossing branches, weak stems.*

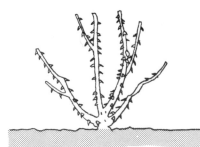

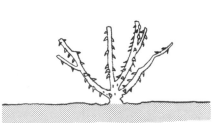

Prune standard rose *to keep top open and symmetrical, and to remove twigs.*

In mild winter climates, *cut back canes as shown at left, so two-thirds of plant remains. In harsh climates, cut back a half to two-thirds.*

Cut old canes *flush with bud union as shown at right. If you leave a stub as shown at left, then rotting stub may damage the entire plant.*

Cut spurs *along canes of climbers so two or three good buds remain.*

APPLE, PEAR, CHERRY

Horizontal branch

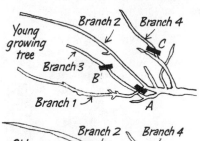

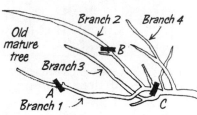

Young growing tree, *length being increased: Cut A removes branch 1, potentially weak. Branch 2 is left intact to grow in length. Cuts B, C subdue branches 3, 4, make branch 2 dominant.* **Mature tree,** *size being maintained: Cut A removes last season's growth, maintains length. Cut B subdues branch 2 in favor of branch 1. On older tree, Cut C helps stimulate replacement wood, not add to length.*

Vertical branch

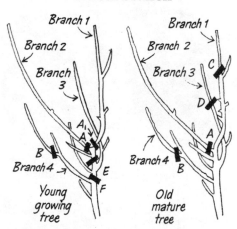

Young growing tree, *length being extended: Make a cut at A or A1, depending on which direction you want growth to go. Remaining branch will become the leader. Cut B heads back branch 4 to help make branch 1 or 2 dominant.* **Old mature tree,** *size being maintained: All cuts made here—A, B, C, and D—are to hold back length. They leave no main branch intact, so none of them will dominate.*

PEACH, NECTARINE

Horizontal branch

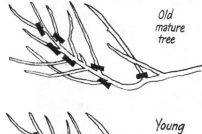

Mature tree: *Cuts marked here remove 2 out of every 3 side branches formed last year (rule for pruning these trees is to remove ⅔ of last year's growth). This is a thinning operation.* **Young growing tree:** *To shorten, cut at either A or B, depending on how much you want to shorten it. This is another way to remove ⅔ of last year's growth and at same time direct growth of the tree into selected branches.*

Vertical branch

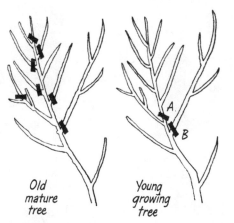

Old mature tree: *Cuts shown here are primarily thinning-out cuts. They do not increase the branch length.* **Young growing tree:** *Here, as in the horizontal branch on the young tree above, cuts A and B will shorten branch and direct growth into selected branches that remain. These cuts would direct growth to the left. This kind of pruning is also good practice on very vigorous growing trees of any age.*

APRICOT, PLUM

Horizontal branch

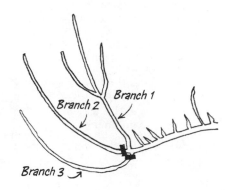

Horizontal branch: *The two lower branches (2 and 3) should be removed, especially on apricot which tends to "come down" with age. These trees form fruit partly on spurs (short, stubby branches growing off main branch at right) and partly on last year's shoots (branches 1, 2, and 3). The spurs bear fruit for several years. The shoots form spurs for next year the same year they bear the fruit.*

Vertical branch

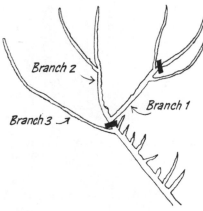

Vertical branch: *Cut at center of drawing would remove branches 1 and 2— typically the best cut to make here, especially if you want to send growth outward and make the tree more spreading. Or, instead of making that cut, you could cut at A to subdue branch 1 so branch 2 could maintain its advantage. Reducing the amount of wood in branches 1, 2, and 3 forces more growth into fewer buds.*

Vines and how to train them

Vines can be used in so many different ways that it's difficult to summarize all their good points. You'll find vines that produce vegetables, flowers for cutting, or flowers for display. Some vines have striking foliage, both evergreen and deciduous. Others bear fruit ranging from the grape to the green-fleshed kiwi.

In landscaping, vines are often usable in places where no other plant has room to grow. A long, blank, sun-baked wall with a walk beside it can be softened or covered with a vine. And a vine growing on a fence gives some of the effect of a hedge but requires less space and maintenance.

Before planting a vine, you should know how fast and how far it will grow. Listed in the opposite column are some of the more common vines, with comments as to special characteristics.

Annuals. Chayote (quick dense cover, squashlike edible fruit); moonflower (flowers); morning glory (flowers); scarlet runner (massed red-orange flowers, edible beans); sweet pea (scented cutting flowers).

Flowers in masses. Bougainvillea; Burmese honeysuckle; clematis; Hall's Japanese honeysuckle (perfume); passion flower; trumpet vines; wisteria (perfume).

Deciduous vines. Bittersweet (attractive orange seeds); Boston ivy (autumn color); grape (fruit); kiwi (fruit; very tender); Virginia creeper (autumn color).

Evergreen vines. Algerian ivy (green or variegated); creeping fig; English ivy (many leaf sizes, shapes).

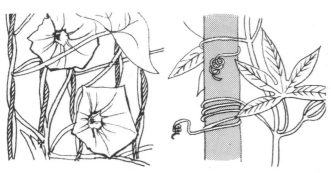

Some stems twine around vertical support as does morning glory at left. Tendrils of passion vine (right) or peas will twist around any object they touch.

Dislike suckers of plants like Boston ivy or Virginia creeper clamp on to any rough surface. Tiny rootlets along stems of many kinds of ivy attach themselves to wall.

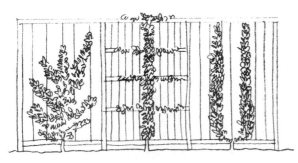

Train vines on a fence by attaching ends to wood strips or securing them with wire; make whatever pattern you like.

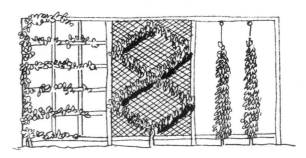

Lattice screens, or wood and wire frames, keep vines growing where you want them for privacy, windbreaks.

Hinged trellis of vines (left) can be pulled back for painting wall. Wires attached to post help weak climbers.

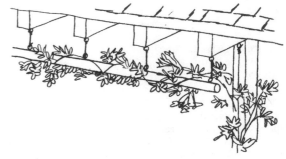

Vine-draped dowel hung from eaves helps to soften the line of the eaves. Attach dowel with wire or pins.

The art of espaliering

Espaliering—the training of a plant into a definite pattern—is an exacting but rewarding art. Many kinds of plants can be espaliered, with variation of technique.

The drawings below show you how to espalier a fruit tree. Fruit trees are most often the subject for espaliering, and for good reason: Espaliering exposes a maximum of branch surface to the sun, and, therefore, stimulates heavier flower and fruit production. Apples, pears, apricots, cherries, and plums are all favorite espalier subjects. Dwarf forms of all five are available, and are a good choice for smaller gardens.

If you live in a cool climate, choose a planting site against a south wall or fence. In hot-summer regions, give plants an eastern exposure so reflected heat won't burn the fruit.

Supports must be sturdy, because branches are heavy when loaded with fruit. Use posts of galvanized pipe or wood (4 by 4-inch), with 14-gage galvanized wire stretched tightly on turnbuckles. Leave 4 to 12 inches between the trellis and wall for free air circulation and for working room.

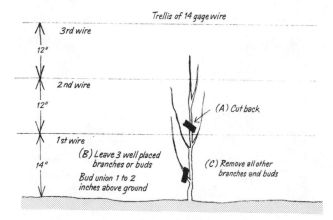

1. Planting time. *Newly planted tree rests against wire support. Wire should be strung north to south if possible, and should have turnbuckles for tightening when wire sags. Remove all but first tier branches; tie these to wire.*

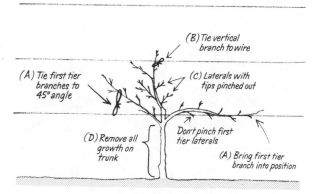

2. First growing season. *Gradually train first tier of branches to horizontal position and tie the growing vertical to the next wire. Choose two young branches for next tier and pinch tips of any others.*

Train the first pair of cordons (horizontal branches) to the wire about 14 inches above the ground. Space other branches about a foot higher.

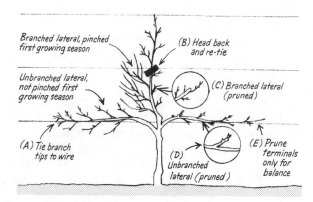

3. Head back vertical *below second wire when tree loses leaves. Leave two branches for second tier and cut back any others to stubs with two or three spurs. Stubs will eventually produce fruit along trunk.*

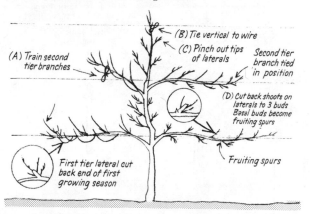

4. Second growing season. Train second tier branches as you did first tier during first growing season. Fruiting spurs will form at base of all laterals below second tier; will produce fruit in a year.

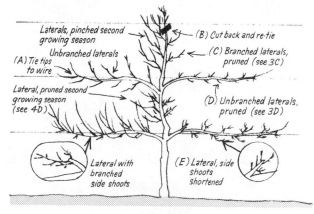

5. Second dormant season. Head back vertical branch below third wire. Prune second tier laterals as you did first tier during first dormant season. Continue training in succeeding years, keeping tree to shape.

SUMMER HEAT, WINTER COLD
...how to protect plants from extreme weather

Gardeners often want to plant something that isn't suited to their natural climate. If you live in a cold region, for example, you may dream of having a warm-climate plant such as an orange or lemon. Or, if you live in the desert, your wish may be to grow moisture-loving plants such as fuchsias and begonias.

A number of devices can be used to produce an artificial climate for the plant you wish to grow— from a simple, temporary structure such as a sunshade or frost protector to a more elaborate lath structure or greenhouse. The purpose of any such covering is to simulate the natural needs of each plant, whether for greater warmth, higher humidity, dense shade, or wind protection.

Sometimes you can provide special climate conditions without using a protective covering. For example, in cool-summer climates you can plant fruit trees against a south-facing masonry wall; it will provide the extra warmth required to ripen the fruit by retaining heat at night and reflecting it during the day.

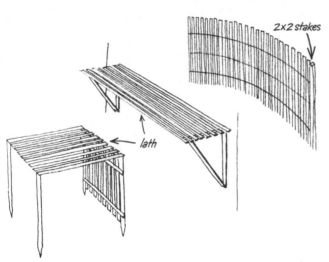

Simple shades *of lath and bean poles or lath and wire fencing give plants temporary protection from hot sun.*

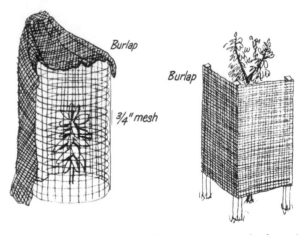

Wire cylinder *draped with burlap acts as shade, windbreak. For tall-trunked plant, use burlap tacked to stakes.*

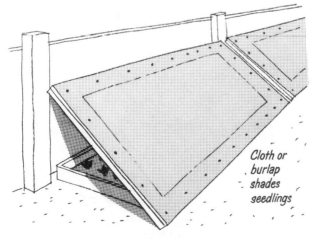

Tacked burlap *over propped-up lath or stake frame shades flats or seedlings or new transplants in ground.*

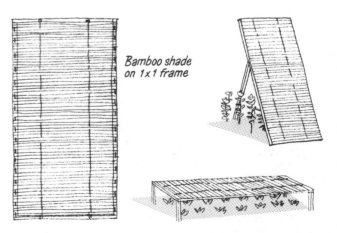

Roll shades *of plastic or bamboo come in many widths, lengths. Use various kinds of pole frames for support.*

FOR TOO MUCH SUN—SUNSHADES

The sketches on these two pages illustrate a number of simple-to-make sunshades. All are easy to move; most come apart for efficient storage.

Look for readymade material when building sunshades. The lath and wire fencing and bamboo blinds shown on the opposite page are examples. You can also buy inexpensive reed fencing, or plastic blinds.

For a permanent planting of shade-loving plants, you might consider building a roof over a patio or along a fence or wall, using either lath or some of the plastic or metal panels available. You may even want to build a completely enclosed lath shelter.

If the shelter you choose is just a roof, try to face it to the east or north and cut off all light from the south and west. The sketch below shows the reason. Early morning sun

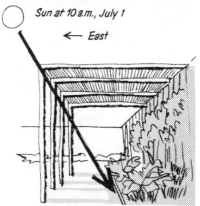

Overhang shades *plants from midmorning sun; admits early morning sun.*

will shine into the shelter while the air is still cool, stimulating bloom and good leaf color. Then as the sun climbs higher and air temperatures rise, the roof will protect the plants.

Where you have no choice and must face the covering to the south, the overhang will have to be deeper to provide shade in late summer and early fall when the sun is low in the sky. Before building, check on the width of roof you'll need by standing an 8-foot pole vertically at the spot where you want the overhang to end. Do it in late September when the sun has dropped lower in the sky but the air is still warm, and note where the pole's shadow stops. Sun will penetrate that far into your shelter at that time of year. By December it will penetrate still farther, but the air will be colder.

1. Build frame *of 1 by 4s with diagonal crossbar. Top and bottom strips extend 6 inches beyond side strips.*

2. Cover frame *with lath strips, using a post along one side to help in lining them up evenly before nailing them.*

3. Nail down *alternate lath strips. To build a 6-foot shade frame you'll need about 22 nailed strips.*

4. Remove loose strips, *then nail each lath to diagonal crossbar. Attach to legs or prop against fence.*

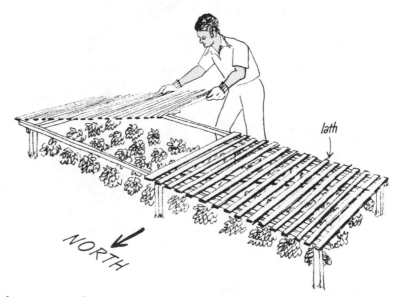

Lath screen *on 1 by 4 frame can be placed over beds of new seedlings as shown here, or you can prop it up on south side of a planting bed.*

Cold weather protection

Protecting plants from cold weather is second nature to gardeners in regions where winter means snow and zero degree weather. Roses and other plants that can't take the cold are bundled up or buried under piles of leaves or straw. Container plants are moved to sheltered locations. Outside pipes are drained and water is turned off.

In mild-winter regions where frosts and occasional hard freezes occur, gardeners are not as likely to be winter-conscious. They may grow many semi-hardy and tender plants that thrive in their climate, and quite frequently several winters will pass with no damage whatsoever. Then along comes a winter with temperatures dipping to just a few degrees lower; this is when unprotected plants can be killed.

A hard, ruinous frost seldom strikes completely unexpectedly. There are almost always several nights of light frost—the kind that nips but doesn't kill—before you get a frost that really means business. You can trace the pattern of danger by watching for any areas where plant foliage has been nipped or for frosted stretches of lawn or bare earth, and know pretty well where frost will strike later on.

The most likely spots to be hit by frost are stretches of open ground exposed to the sky on all sides, particularly to the north sky. Plants in hollows or in enclosed areas where cold air is held motionless are also in danger.

Regardless of what kind of shelter you use to protect your garden from extreme cold, be sure to keep the soil damp around plants.

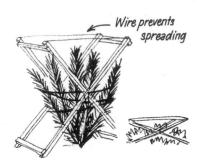

Portable frost shelter *opens wider for larger plants; can be covered with plastic, cloth, burlap; folds to store.*

Small coldframe *(see others, pages 90-91) protects young plants. Electric cable in soil keeps heat constant.*

Lath frame *for frost covering is not eyesore if you leave it in place for winter. Cover at night.*

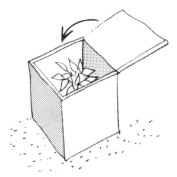

Cardboard or wooden box *is bottomless; hinged top can be opened during the day to admit air, light.*

Push ends of bamboo frame into soil

Bamboo stakes *make a tent frame for a plastic cover. Keep plastic in place with rocks, or bury the bottom edge.*

Wire coat hangers *were bent into a handy frame for frost cover. Rustproof paint makes them last longer.*

Paraffin-treated paper *makes a "hot-cap." Sun warms soil; trapped heat keeps plants warm at night.*

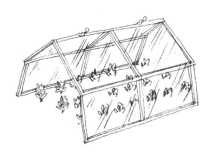

Cloches, *made of double-strength glass, are attached together to protect seedlings at night, trap day heat.*

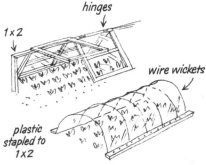

Old window sashes *or plastic attached to wood or wire frames protect plants against light frosts.*

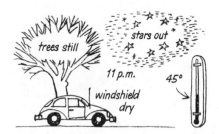

Check at bedtime *for signs that hard frost is on the way; cover any tender plants until temperatures rise.*

Evergreen branches break *under snow loads. To prevent this, brush off or shake branches to remove snow.*

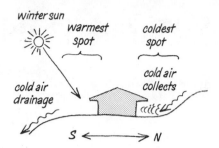

Hillside gardens *often have several climate zones. Cold air "drains" on slope, collects in low, enclosed places.*

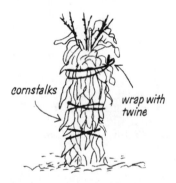

Exposed plants *are quickly damaged by frost. Protective eaves will prevent damage if cold not extreme.*

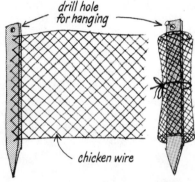

Open-ended *frame can be covered with heavy plastic or burlap to make a temporary winter greenhouse.*

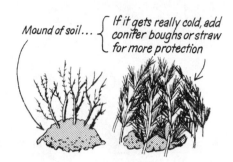

Protect roses *where ground freezes by mounding soil over trunk or covering entire plant with boughs or straw.*

Insulate taller roses *against hard freezes by wrapping them with cornstalks; secure with twine or rope.*

Tack chicken wire *to a stake, using wire as tall as your plant and long enough to form cylinder around plant. Put stake into ground next to plant, circle plant with wire, and secure the ends. Pack cylinder with straw.*

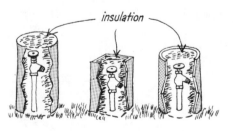

Protect pipes *and faucets in hard freeze by covering with cans, boxes, or tile filled with insulation.*

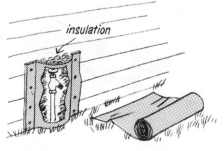

Tack tar paper *to wall and fill with peat moss, fiberglass, or other insulation to protect pipes, faucets.*

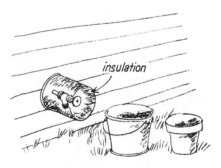

Other pipe coverings *can be cans, buckets, clay pots filled with insulation. Or, wrap with sacks or towels.*

Coldframes and hotbeds

Experienced gardeners consider a coldframe as an indispensable tool to successful year-round gardening. In fact to many, a well-built, well-tended coldframe is nearly as useful as a small greenhouse. And it takes up far less space and can cost almost nothing if you build it with scrap lumber.

A useful coldframe can be anything from a simple frame with a cover of plastic sheeting to a more elaborate structure with its own heat source. You may want to start with something fairly simple until you see just how much you'll use it. But if you are handy with tools you might consider building the large coldframe shown at the bottom of the page. It will take you a day to put it together—maybe even less time if you have some old windows or a glass door on hand.

FOR COLD OR HOT WEATHER

In milder climates, coldframes protect plants against frost and help to keep temperatures warm enough for proper plant growth through the winter. In cold winter regions, they give the same results provided the unit has an auxiliary heating system. If so, the structure is commonly known as a "hotbed." The text on these two pages uses the term coldframe exclusively; however, if you live in a cold climate, the term also means "hotbed."

Whatever the climate, a coldframe is especially useful for early planting of summer annuals and seeds, protecting tender plants in winter, forcing cuttings to root faster, starting perennials from seed in summer, and growing many kinds of plants you wouldn't otherwise attempt to grow.

How can a structure consisting of four walls with a transparent roof make all this possible? The answer is that a coldframe acts as a controlled weather capsule in which temperature, humidity, and light are kept within the limits favorable for plant growth. In addition, it protects tender seedlings and cuttings from attacks by pests and birds and from damage by wind or hail.

WHAT HAPPENS INSIDE

A coldframe traps heat by admitting sunlight during the day through its transparent covering of glass or plastic, and retaining heat radiated from the surrounding soil during the cool night hours. Also, the nearly airtight structure keeps loss of moisture through evaporation to a minimum—and cuts down on your watering chores. The simplest piece of garden equipment that employs this principle of a heat and moisture trap is the "hotcap," a dome of heavy waxed paper used to protect tomatoes,

melons, and other young plants from the possibility of late spring frosts.

FIRST, ROUGH-OUT A PLAN

In planning a coldframe, start with the dimensions of the cover. If you are not restricted to a certain size, choose dimensions that will fit some multiple of a standard planting flat. Flats come in several sizes, but two commonly used types measure 14½ by 23½ inches and 18½ by 18½ inches. Make your frame with enough leeway so you can lift flats in and out without pinching fingers.

If you want to use scrap pieces of lumber and glass you have on hand, then the size of your coldframe will be dictated by the dimensions of these pieces. (You can also buy ready-made sash, usually 3 by 6 feet, or snap together aluminum sash in which you install polyethylene plastic.)

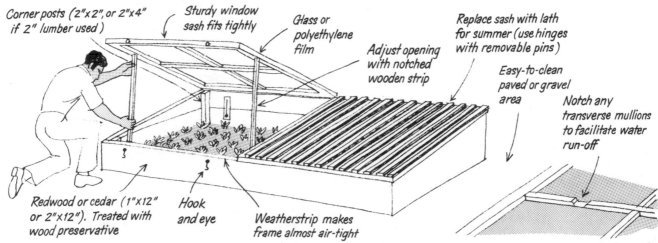

Large coldframe substitutes for greenhouse in a small garden. In hot weather you prop the glass cover open to let excess heat escape (thermometer hung at rear should stay near 80 degrees). Lath cover or whitewashed glass also keeps heat down. In cold weather and at night you shut cover to trap heat, helping to force rapid growth.

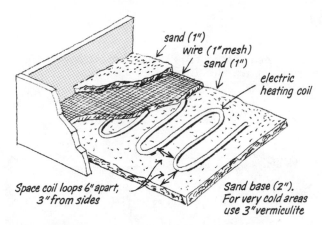

sand (1")
wire (1" mesh)
sand (1")

electric
heating coil

Space coil loops 6" apart,
3" from sides

Sand base (2").
For very cold areas
use 3" vermiculite

Electric heating cable *buried under sand and wire in cold-frame protects plants from freezing temperatures.*

The walls can be made of scrap lumber, or you can buy the cheapest grade of new lumber. Redwood and cedar are long lasting and rot and insect resistant; other types of wood can also be used if you treat them with a preservative. Either 1 by 12 or 2 by 12 lumber is practical. Fit the corners as tightly as you can; or, to make sure no heat escapes, caulk the edges with asphalt emulsion.

BUILDING HINTS

Because the coldframe is heated by the sun, you must slope the cover toward the south. If you can, build the structure so there is a wall or fence on the north side; you'll protect the frame from winds and cut down on loss of heat. To increase the light level within the frame, paint the fence or wall a light color, or paint the cold-frame interior sidewalls white or silver.

Whatever location you choose for your coldframe, make sure it's not in a part of the garden that has poor drainage, since you don't want water to collect around or in the frame after every rain.

OTHER EQUIPMENT YOU'LL NEED

A good thermometer is essential if you want your cold-frame to work. Most plants that will grow well outdoors in North America will continue growing at temperatures from about 40° to 100°, and do best at about 85°. When your thermometer reaches 85°, you can prop open the top of the frame to let out some heat. Then in late afternoon, when the outside temperature starts to fall, shut the top to trap the heat radiated by the soil. In really hot weather you'll have to whitewash the glass, or make a second cover of lath to cut down on the light.

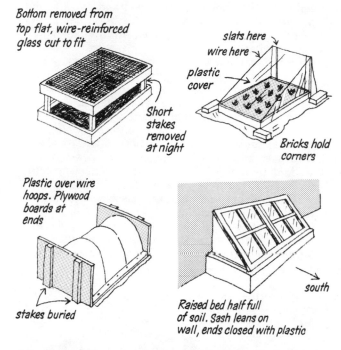

Bottom removed from
top flat, wire-reinforced
glass cut to fit

Short
stakes
removed
at night

slats here
wire here
plastic
cover

Bricks hold
corners

Plastic over wire
hoops. Plywood
boards at
ends

stakes buried

Raised bed half full
of soil. Sash leans on
wall, ends closed with plastic

south

Adapting coldframe principle *to a flat, a raised bed or just a few seedlings is easy. Use a cover similar to those above during cold periods. In midwinter these structures won't work because air volume is small, no heat is supplied.*

Open sash to
lower temperature
and humidity

Thermometer

Mist cools
air, raises
humidity

Large glass area for
maximum sunlight

Use whitewash or
a cloth shade in very
hot weather

Tight fit to hold
heat and moisture

Wall reflects
sunlight, shields
frame from
winter wind

Soil absorbs sun's heat,
gives it off at night. Close
sash and cover with blanket
on frosty nights

South

Coldframe cover *acts as a heat trap. Light passes through, but long infrared rays cannot escape. With top shut, heat increases. To lower temperature in summer, use a mist* nozzle and very light flow of water. To retain trapped soil heat on cold winter nights, cover the glass with a blanket, board, or other insulating material.

Simple ways to beat the frost

A few balmy days in late winter or early spring can trick even an experienced gardener into setting out plants or sowing some seed too early.

You can make temporary coverings for tender plants, and even make them grow faster than normal. Use any one of the four ideas illustrated below or use your imagination and the materials you have on hand to create different coverings.

The umbrellalike objects shown below are in fact umbrellas—the plastic kind that come down around your shoulders. The handles were removed and glued to the top; the sharp center rod sticks into the ground. This type of covering should be removed briefly once a day so air can circulate.

The miniature, one-plant greenhouses shown at lower right were made from glass jugs. You can buy kits with which to remove the bottoms or try this method: Soak a piece of coarse twine in kerosene, tie it around the bottom of the bottle, and light it with a match. When it burns out, quickly plunge the bottle into cold water; the bottom will break off. Once the bottles are in place, you can leave the tops off for air circulation; be sure to replace them on nights when you expect damaging cold.

You can make the same type of coverings with plastic bottles. Cut off the bottoms with scissors. The bottles must be removed during the day to admit light.

Frame coverings like the ones shown at right are made with lumber scraps, even broken bean poles and lath strips. Cover the frame with a plastic drop cloth or an old bed sheet. When temperatures become warm enough, remove the frame. For cucumbers you can leave the frame (minus the covering) shown in the sketch to support the plants during the summer; they will spread over the top.

Wood frame *with plastic cover on top and around 3 sides gives seedlings head start. Cover open side at night.*

Bean pole legs *support lengths of lath to make frame for plastic covering. Frame supports vines later.*

Bottomless bottles *with caps removed help produce warmth for seedlings during the day. Replace caps at night.*

Giant "hotcap" *is just a plastic umbrella with handle removed and placed on top; shaft is anchored in soil.*

Planting in warm weather

In most regions, you can plant in spring and fall. You can even plant bare root shrubs and trees in midwinter in many areas. But, what if you live in a desert region where it's always warm or you just can't manage to plant any other time but summer? The answer is simple: Go ahead and plant regardless of high temperatures, but be sure to take the proper precautions.

The illustrations below show how some nurserymen and landscape contractors in desert regions plant nursery trees and shrubs during the summer. At first glance you might think the steps involved are just what you would do any time; but notice the lavish use of water in nearly every step. You must water the planting hole and the ground around it, the soil mix used for backfill (don't make it soggy), the root ball of the plant while it's still in the container, and the soil mix as it goes into the hole.

Finally you water the plant after it is settled and a watering basin is formed. (*Caution:* You will be working with soaked soil and wet backfill. Be especially careful not to pack it as you dig and refill the hole—you could easily create a hard shell around the rootball that roots would have trouble penetrating.)

All plants set out in warm weather should be protected from wind and sun with a temporary shade of lath or burlap. Be especially careful to cover the exposures to the south and the west. If you use burlap, moisten it when the wind blows to make a type of air conditioner.

One other precaution: If you can, plant just before or after the sun goes down. The plant has the long cool night in which to take up moisture before the heat of the next day begins.

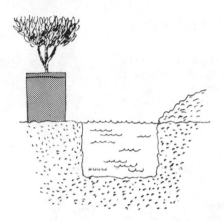

1. Dig planting hole *and fill with water. Let water drain thoroughly before continuing. Also moisten the soil you removed and let it dry a bit as the hole drains. Be careful not to compact any of the soil as you are working.*

2. Moisten soil amendment *(a quantity that would fill half the planting hole). Peat moss must be kneaded with water, then squeezed dry. Toss amendment with equal volume of moist soil to mix without compacting.*

3. Water plant thoroughly, *then let it drain. While you're waiting, place a layer of amended backfill in the hole and mix in a tablespoonful of superphosphate to insure proper root growth. Level the backfill.*

4. Place plant *in hole so top of container soil is level with the ground. With water running slowly into the the hole, spade backfill evenly around plant. Don't let water run in so fast that it can't drain away quickly.*

5. Finish filling hole *and form watering basin by mounding soil around the plant. Fill the basin with water several times and let it drain. Water will keep plant moist until the roots have a chance to take hold.*

6. Pile mulch, *3 inches thick, in, over, and around watering basin. Use ground fir bark, moist peat moss, or nitrogen stabilized sawdust. In a week to 10 days, remove mulch from trunk of plant so trunk won't rot.*

GARDEN TOOLS
...buying, maintaining, and repairing

A new home owner, about to buy his first garden tools, may find the display of tools in nursery supply centers and hardware stores somewhat bewildering. Does gardening require such an arsenal? Which ones are necessary? What should you know about them?

DON'T BUY ALL YOUR TOOLS AT ONCE

If you follow your hunches, and buy the most familiar forms—shovel, rake, and hoe—you'll be right. But how about all the other tools offered? Actually, most of these were originally introduced to do specific agricultural jobs, but sometimes a home gardener found other functions for one or two of them, or the manufacturer altered a tool's design to fit the home gardener's needs. The asparagus knife, for example, makes a dandy weeder, and the Warren hoe, originally designed for making furrows and for seeding operations, is now used more in home gardens for cultivating around shrubs.

CHOOSE TOOLS CAREFULLY

Tools are very personal pieces of equipment and all experienced gardeners have their favorites. Sunset's editors asked home gardeners to evaluate some of the most widely used tools such as the shovel, rake, and hoe. Their answers show little agreement in tool choice but hint at the versatility of most tools. For example, on the lawn rake: "The metal fan-shaped rake is ideal for collecting grass clippings . . . I like the light, easy surface touch of the bamboo rake . . . Give me the bamboo rake every time." Or on trowels: "An all-metal trowel will last forever . . . A trowel with a wood handle is less likely to raise blisters . . . My wood-handled trowel has lasted 22 years and is still going strong . . . If a trowel doesn't feel like part of your hand, throw it out."

In the text accompanying the sketches of tools, no attempt is made to judge whether a tool is good or bad. Your work habits, your plants, your strength, and your stature will determine which tools work most efficiently for you. Tools shown on these three pages are those most commonly used. You won't find any of the very specialized tools, or power tools, or lawn clippers and edgers.

It's not likely that a gardener would buy all the tools shown, because many perform the same function. However, when you buy garden tools, get the very best you can afford. A top quality product, if properly taken care of, will last you through most of your gardening years.

Don't buy any tool until you have checked it over thoroughly. Lift and swing the piece of equipment around a bit to test its weight and proper balance. A man-sized hoe may be just right for you but too heavy for anyone else in the family. How about handle length?

You may feel that a long-handled spade or fork is easier to wield. (It's a good idea to take along all the gardening members of the family when you're out buying garden tools.) Try the grip on all small hand tools. Get the one that "feels right" in your hand.

SHOVELS

Long handle, round point. A versatile tool for digging and scooping. The round-point irrigation shovel (see sketch of two shovels at right) has a straighter shank, which gives it more strength and makes it better for digging planting holes or ditches with vertical sides.

Long handle, square point. For leveling areas for patios and walks, squaring off the bottoms of ditches, and shoveling snow. When shoveling dirt or gravel, this shovel is especially handy when you get toward the bottom of the pile.

D-handle shovels. For jobs such as moving soil, sand, gravel, and for picking up litter. Round point and square point models are available.

Square end spade. For edging, digging, and cultivating (see page 12). This tool is easy to handle. You have a choice of a long handle or the shorter D-handle. Always sharpen a spade before you use it.

Garden shovel. Somewhat smaller and lighter than the regular round point shovel. A convenient shovel for a women gardener. Use it for digging holes, cultivating, and edging. It can be used with a chopping motion to break up earth clods.

Transplanting spade. A favorite with gardeners for transplanting shrubs and moving perennials.

Scoop shovel. For moving sawdust, manure, and other light materials. Serves as a garden dust pan for collecting litter.

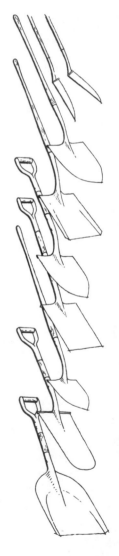

HOES

Garden hoes. There are hoes for just about every job. The 6-inch-wide hoe is the most commonly used. Other types include a 2½-inch-wide blade for light jobs in narrow spots, an 8-inch-wide blade for driveways and walks, and special kinds with names that suggest their use: planter hoe, cotton hoe, square top onion hoe. The latter, also called a strawberry hoe, has a blade 7 inches wide and about 1¾ inches high; use around shallow rooted plants. To be effective, a hoe should be sharpened each time you take it into the garden. On hard cutting jobs, resharpen about every two hours.

Hoes with the conventional design of those illustrated at right work best with a chopping action, the flat front edges cutting weeds off at ground level, or the sharp edges working like a small pick. Get a hoe that is light enough to be wielded for an hour or two at a time.

Push-pull weeder-cultivator. One of many variations on the scuffle hoe. You scrape the surface of a bed, cutting off seedling weeds and breaking the soil crust. This one wobbles as you change directions so the blade is always at the proper angle. Other varieties have a blade shaped as a flat rectangle, a double disc, or a golf iron.

Warren hoe. For cultivating between plants or for making furrows. You make the furrow with the pointed end, seed, then turn the hoe over and use the "ears" to pull the soil over the seed.

Weeding hoe. Hoe on one side, weed puller on the other.

SHEARS

Hedge shears. For shaping hedges, shrubs; cutting or shearing back perennials, ground covers, and faded flower heads. Some models have built-in shock absorbers. Hedge shears are not a substitute for pruning shears. They won't cut through thick stems or branches.

Lopping shears. Essential for pruning branches smaller in diameter than a broom handle. The long handle gives you greater cutting and reaching power. Handles are 20 to 24 inches long.

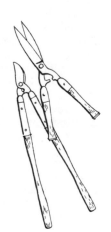

Pruning shears. Probably the most consistently used of all garden tools. Also available, in addition to anvil and hook-and-blade types, are special rose pruning shears and shears for cutting flowers. Buy a model that fits your hand.

SPADING FORKS

Long handle spading fork. Long handle gives good leverage when you are working in hard soil. Breaks up adobe clods better than a spade. Buy the best quality fork; otherwise, tines may bend.

Short handle fork. You have a choice of a number of models. Tines range from 7 to 11 inches long. Weight also varies. Get the model that's right for you. Generally, short handled spading forks work best in crowded planting beds or to lift clumps of perennials without damaging the tubers, rhizomes, or a plant's fleshy or thick matted root system.

Barn or manure fork. Not for spading, but for moving garden prunings, long weeds, manure, and other materials that hang together. Also good for turning over layers of compost.

SPECIAL TOOLS

Cultivators. Good for breaking up hard soil around plants. They won't qualify for deep spading. For best results, combine chopping and pulling motions.

Weed and grass cutters. Weed cutter is used for rugged weeds and grasses in uncultivated garden areas. It removes top growth but not weed roots, unless you use blade as a chopper. Grass cutter helps in cutting grass along the edge of a lawn. Swing it as you would a golf club. Test various models for correct balance and weight.

Trowel. One of the most personal of all garden tools. Shop around until you get one that fits your hand, is well-balanced, and light enough to handle easily. A straight shank model is good for bulb planting. Drop shank is most popular.

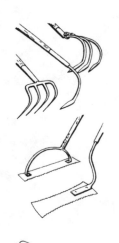

(Continued on next page)

Asparagus or dandelion weeders. For lifting out tap-rooted weeds in the garden and for weeding in such tight places as between stepping-stones in a path. These tools are useful, too, for small cultivating jobs.

Small hand cultivators and hoes. For close-up kneeling or sitting jobs or for planting on a hillside. The end of these cultivators is the same shape and design as that of regular-sized tools, but they are smaller, with palm-sized handles.

Mattock. Wide blade, similar to a heavy hoe, smashes through hard, root-filled soil. Use it for bushy weeds, invasive tree roots, spreading ground cover. If the end opposite the hoe is an ax, you can use it to trim ivy edges or cut side roots in tree and bush removal.

RAKES

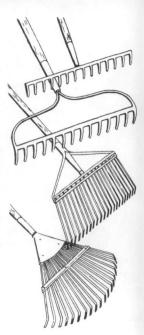

Level head rakes. Flat top used to level seed beds and make seed furrows. It won't do the heavy work the bow rake will.

Metal bow rake. Good tool for leveling soil or gravel and collecting earth clods. The bow acts as a shock absorber, giving the rake a springy, resilient quality.

Lawn rake. Indispensable for raking lawn clippings, leaves, and other light matter on both paved and natural surfaces. You have a wide selection to choose from. Some are made of metal, others of bamboo; some are fan-shaped, others rectangular. On some models you can adjust the width of the raking face.

New handles for old tools

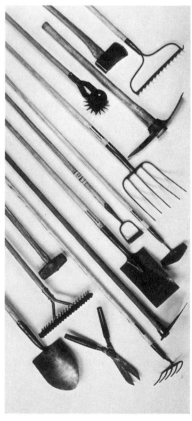

Rusty, broken garden tools *can be fixed by replacing handles and cleaning metal parts (see photos on next page).*

Years of hard use and exposure to the elements may result in the handles of your garden tools wearing away until they eventually break. If this happens to you, don't automatically throw the tool away. Most likely, the handle can be repaired or replaced for quite a bit less than the price of a new tool. (Broken metal parts usually are too costly to repair.)

IT'S EASY TO REPLACE

Hardware stores or garden centers stock replacement handles for most popular tools. To make sure the handle will fit properly, take the broken tool along when you go shopping. Also, be sure to buy the necessary hardware to keep the new handle in place—another good reason to take the broken tool with you when shopping.

Replacing the handle is easy if you follow these steps: First, remove the broken part. If the tool head is attached by metal pins, pull them out with hammer-head tongs or large pliers. Rivets can be removed by chopping them off with a cold chisel, by grinding the head down and punching out the shank, or by drilling the heads out using an electric drill (a useful tool for replacing all kinds of tool handles). If the handle fits into a ferrule, use a dowel to knock the tool head off (see photo on opposite page). A broken handle in a curved socket (like those found in many shovels) is not as easy to remove. You'll have to drill out all the wood you can with an electric drill, then pick out the fragments with pliers. (*Caution:* Don't burn out wood fragments; heat will spoil the temper of the steel head).

To put a new handle into a curved socket, you'll have to soak the end of the new handle in water for two or three hours. This will soften the wood enough so you can put the handle end in the socket. Stand handle on a masonry floor or other hard surface, fit the tool socket over the softened end, and hold the socket in place while you pound the handle end on the floor to drive the wet wood into place.

Once the new handle is in place, your next step is to clean up and remove rust spots on the metal tool head with emery paper, a disc sander, or a wire brush. Then sharpen the cutting edge with a file, a sharpening stone, or an electric drill with an abrasive disc.

PREVENTIVE MAINTENANCE

Keeping your tools or new tool parts in good shape will help to prevent breakage. For a spade, hoe, or other cutting tool, keep the cutting edge sharp. A sharp blade not only makes normal digging or hoeing go faster, but also helps to cut through those roots you'd like to keep from spreading. To keep a metal tool head rust-free, submerge it in a bucket of oily sand after each use.

Wooden handles will last longer if you keep them stored indoors. Also, rubbing the handles with a little linseed oil will help keep the wood from drying out, preventing it from shrinking or splitting.

Remove ferrule *from a hoe by clamping tool shank in place and using dowel as a lever; pound with hammer.*

Use an electric drill *to remove wood fragments from a curved socket, or to drill out heads of metal rivets.*

Disc sander *fits into electric drill, sharpens dull mattock quickly. Use goggles to protect your eyes.*

Pound new rivets *after inserting a new handle and drilling holes through the socket and wood; use anvil to steady.*

Wire wheel *fits electric drill, removes dirt, rust quickly with little effort and no damage to good metal.*

ANNUALS
...colorful plants that grow for only one season

Strictly speaking, the word "annual" means the plant will grow for only one season, then die. Where winters are mild, plant spring blooming annuals in the fall; in other climates, plant them in early spring. Summer blooming annuals should be planted in spring after the last frost. Whatever the climate, all annuals should be planted in full sun unless the listings for individual plants given below recommend another location.

Spring blooming annuals

African daisy
Flowers are white (or white with violet markings), yellow, or salmon on 6 to 12-inch stems which rise from low plants.

Alyssum
Masses of tiny flowers in white, red, or violet. Use for quick ground cover in a bulb bed or as a low border.

Calendula
Big yellow or orange flowers on stems to 24 inches. Make good cut flowers. Blooms in winter in warm climates.

California poppy
Orange, red, or white flowers on feathery plants. Plant in informal groups. Plants may reseed themselves in warm areas.

Candytuft
White and pastel-clustered flowers on plants from 6 to 15 inches tall. Group together; use as cover for bulb bed.

Canterbury bells
Flowers in blue, purple, pink, white on plants from 2½ to 4 feet tall. Set out in spring. Some make good hanging plants.

Centaurea
Bachelor's button has flowers in red, blue, white on stems to 2½ feet tall. Use as background plants for low-growing annuals.

Cineraria
Clusters of daisylike flowers in blue, violet, pink, white. Has lush foliage. Grows best in cool shade. Will reseed itself.

Forget-me-not
Sprays of tiny blue or white flowers to 2 feet tall. Plant in shaded areas. Good planted under flowering shrubs.

Larkspur
Flowers in blues, white, rose, lilac on stalks to 4 feet tall. If stalks need support, tie to bamboo stakes. Good in background.

Layia
Yellow flowers are daisylike with white petal tips; plants grow to 8 inches tall. Will take heavy soil. May reseed itself.

Lupine
Blue, white, and pink flowers on plants from 8 to 18 inches high. Good companion plant to California poppy.

Nemesia
Wide range of brilliant colored flowers on plants from 10 to 18 inches tall. Need rich soil and cool spring weather.

Shirley poppy
White, pink, or red flowers on stems from 2 to 5 inches tall. The petals are crinkly. Remove seed pods to extend bloom.

Snapdragon
Flowers bloom in many colors, grow on spikes from 4 inches to 4 feet. Some forms have open flowers. Plant seeds in fall.

Stock
Many strongly scented flowers in white, red, pink, blues, purple. Plants grow to 2 feet. Make good cut flowers.

Sweet pea
Small, strong-scented flowers in all colors on bushy or climbing vines. Use a net or string to train vines. Good as cut flowers.

Viola
Two types: Pansies have large blooms, variegated in many colors; violas have small flowers in white, blue, yellow.

Summer blooming annuals

Ageratum
Flowers in lavender blue, white, pink on plants from 4 to 18 inches tall. Lower forms are excellent for borders.

Amaranthus
Plants from 4 to 8 feet tall with tassel-like flowers in red or red and green. Plant is somewhat weed-like. A novelty plant.

Aster
Plants grow to 3 feet tall with daisy-shaped blooms in many colors. Plants are disease prone, may be attacked by wilt.

Browallia
Blue, violet, or white flowers on 2-foot stems. Good for cut flowers or in hanging baskets. Order seed from catalogs.

Celosia
Red, yellow, orange plumelike flowers on stems to 3 feet tall. Blooms are like feathers. One variety is velvety crested.

Chrysanthemum
Flowers in yellow, purple, orange. Plants grow to 3 feet tall and to 3 feet across. Are good as long lasting cut flowers.

Summer blooming annuals (cont'd)

Clarkia
White, pink, or red flowers are single or double; bloom at each leaf node. Grows to 18 inches tall. Likes light shade or sun.

Cleome
Flowers in pink and white on plant that may reach 4 feet tall. Can be grown as a hedge. Can take some shade.

Coreopsis
Daisylike flowers in yellow, orange, reddish; some forms are banded. Plants are low growing. Grow from seeds.

Cosmos
Daisylike flowers in white, yellow, pink, rose, purple on plants from 2 to 6 feet tall. Foliage is feathery. Grows from seed.

Dwarf dahlia
Flowers in many colors on plants that grow to 2 feet tall. Plant seeds in spring; tubers will form that you can replant.

Gaillardia
Red, yellow, and gold flowers on tall stems to 2 feet. Stems may need support to stay upright. Plants need warm weather.

Gypsophila
Clusters of short-lived single or double flowers in white, pink, and rose. Plants grow from 6 inches to 4 feet tall.

Hollyhock
Single or double flowers in rose, red, pinks, yellow, white, and apricot; stems to 9 feet tall. Best used in background.

Impatiens
Red, pink, lavender, or white flowers on bushy plants to 2 feet tall. They like sun, light shade. Sometimes called balsam.

Linaria
Flowers that resemble tiny snapdragons in shades of red, blue, purple, yellow, white. Plants grow to 18 inches tall.

Lobelia
White or blue tiny flowers on low growing plants. Good in containers, as borders, or as a cover over bulb beds.

Marigold
Yellow, orange, rust single or pomponlike flowers on stems from a few inches to 3 feet tall. Makes long lasting cut flowers.

Mimulus
Large flowers to 2½ inches across in gold, red, yellow; some are spotted brown, maroon. Needs cool temperatures, shade.

Morning glory
Quick-growing summer vines with short-lived trumpet-shaped flowers in white, blues, and pink. Sow seeds in spring.

Nasturtium
Plants are bushy or vine-like with round lush leaves; from 8 to 15 inches tall. Flowers in maroon, red, orange, yellow.

Nicotiana
Straggling plants are from 1 to 3 feet tall. Flowers in red, lavender, maroon, lime, white have nice scent in evening.

Petunia
Flowers in all colors; can be plain or variegated, single, ruffled, or double. Plant in containers or mass together in beds.

Phlox
Flowers in lavender, pink, red, white, yellow bloom in clusters. Plants from 6 to 18 inches tall. Best planted in groups.

Pinks
Tiny carnation flowers in pink, rose, red, white. Plants grow to 30 inches, have gray-green foliage. Sow seeds in fall, spring.

Portulaca
Flowers in yellow, orange, various reds, white, lavender or magenta. Plants grow to 6 inches tall. Leaves are fleshy.

Scabiosa
Flowers from deep purple to pink, white on stems to 3 feet tall. Good planted in mixed flower bed. Odd-shaped flowers.

Scarlet flax
Brilliant red flowers contrast with gray-green foliage. Plants grow to 18 inches tall. Grow with other gray-leafed plants.

Scarlet sage
Tall, thin, red flower spikes from 8 to 30 inches tall on gray-green plants. Use as a tall border or as background plant.

Statice
Flower clusters come in blue, purple, rose, and yellow on 2-foot stems, rise from low plants. Good as dried flowers.

Strawflower
Flowers with straw-like petals, velvety centers in orange, red, white, yellow. Use dried flowers in winter arrangements.

Sunflower
Tall variety grows to 10 feet tall, has big, disc-shaped yellow flowers with edible seeds. Grow in vegetable garden.

Sweet basil
Foliage plant grows to 24 inches tall. Leaves used as herb for seasoning foods. A purple-leafed form is interesting.

Torenia
Flowers in lavender, purple, blue, white with yellow throats on plants with bronzy green foliage. Needs shade.

Verbena
Flowers in violet, red, cream, and pastels, in clusters on creeping stems. Makes a good ground cover or border plant.

Zinnia
Plants come in all sizes, brilliant colors. Flowers tend to look artificial. Give them plenty of sun, heat, and air.

Planting annuals from containers

Even though many annuals will grow reasonably quickly from seed, there's still the precarious few weeks of contending with weeds, hungry birds, and of keeping the planting bed moist enough for the seeds to sprout. You can avoid all this by selecting nursery plants. Nurtured through the seedling period by professionals with ideal growing conditions, nursery plants are initially strong enough to withstand transplanting to a new environment; they grow extremely fast, and usually are not bothered by pests.

When should you plant? In most regions (except the desert areas of the Southwest) spring is the most popular planting time. The exact time will vary depending on the severity of the winter months and how long you'll be susceptible to an unexpected frost. In mild winter regions, you can plant spring-blooming flowers in late fall while the soil is warm. They make their growth and bloom early.

What should you plant? The answer depends largely on the size of your planting beds, how much time you want to spend caring for your plants, and how much you can afford. Your nurseryman will be able to suggest several ideas to fit your needs. As you are making your choice, keep in mind that for an effective display, tall plants should be placed towards the back of the planting bed with smaller plants in front. Also make sure flower colors will harmonize. To avoid any mistakes, draw a sketch of your planting beds along with approximate dimensions. Place one plant every 6 inches (one every 10 or 12 inches for tall, strong growers). Be sure that plants in flats or containers are lush and compact with little bloom. Leggy plants or those in full bloom have been there too long; you would be wise to choose another plant.

Most flowering plants need lots of sun. If you enjoy indoor displays of cut flowers, plant a special bed out of sight so you can cut at will without spoiling the looks of the garden.

Soil preparation. Spade up and rake your planting beds as shown in the drawings below, adding any necessary amendments (see section on soil amendments, pages 4—7). Don't dig weeds into the soil. Hoe them off and discard them. Using your planting plan, mark the bed with the edge of the rake or a trail of lime or sand to show where different plants will go.

How to plant. Plants in nursery flats should be pulled apart gently (not sliced) to keep root systems fairly well intact. The root ball of plants in plastic containers should be scratched to rough up the soil, otherwise the roots won't grow out into the planting soil. Set the plants in moist soil, gently pressing it around the roots; then water thoroughly. Cool or overcast days are ideal for planting annuals. If you must plant in warm weather, set out the plants in early evening and provide a temporary shade from the next day's heat (see protective shades, pages 86 and 87).

Care after planting. Check frequently for moisture level by poking your finger into the soil next to a plant or two. Until the plants become established, all but the top inch of soil should be kept moist, never wet. To keep moisture in and cut down on weeds, use an inch or more of soil amendment as a mulch over any bare earth (see pages 4—7).

Improve and rake the soil

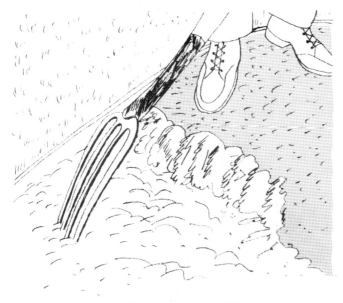

Fork in layer *of amendment and a sprinkling of superphosphate (see pages 5-7 for descriptions of the various amendments). Soak the soil; let it dry out a few days before digging. Break any big clods as you dig.*

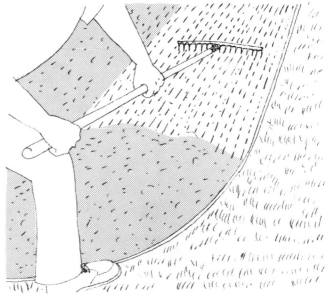

Rake surface, *breaking up smaller clods and picking out rocks, sticks. Use edge of your rake (or a trail of sand) to mark planting areas for different plants. Place small plants in front, tall ones behind.*

Wait a month after planting, then apply a complete fertilizer and water it in thoroughly. In rich soils, one feeding should do for most short season plants. In weaker soils, use a full-strength feeding once a month or a half-strength feeding every two weeks throughout the season. When plants show sturdy new growth, pinch out all the tender tips with thumb and forefinger (see photos on page 79). This will produce bushier growth and more flowers. (Also, if at any time during the growing season a plant becomes straggly, pinch it back.)

If the flowers are allowed to go to seed, fewer new flowers are formed. Remove dead blooms; or, for plants with countless tiny blooms, you can shear them lightly to keep them looking fresh.

Pull plants apart carefully

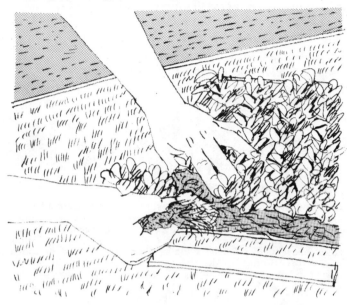

Lift out plants *from a flat without squeezing or you may compact the soil around roots (be sure flat is moist first). Gently pull each plant apart so roots remain intact and point outward from the soil.*

Scratch root ball *of plants taken from plastic containers— they often cause roots to pack at surface of root ball or coil at bottom. Also, cut off any long bottom roots. The roots will grow outward into your garden soil.*

Plant, then cover with a mulch

Dig a hole *just deep enough to hold the plant at the same level as it was in nursery flat or container. Set the plant into the hole; fill with soil, pressing it gently but firmly around the roots.*

Add mulch covering *after planting, using an inch or more of ground fir bark, premoistened peat moss, or nitrogen-stabilized amendment. Mulch will keep weeds down, hold moisture. Water well with fine spray.*

PERENNIALS

...plants that come back year after year

Perennials are those plants that produce new growth at the beginning of each growing season, then bloom for varying periods of time throughout the year. The plants are left in the ground, where they will produce more foliage or die back until the next year. Perennials are versatile plants and can be used for other purposes than just providing flowers for one season. They can be used as low-growing borders, ground covers, foliage plants, quick-growing hedges, or pond or marsh plants.

The listings below and on the next page include 54 perennials, many of which in turn include dozens of plant types, sizes, flower colors, and blooming seasons. Plant perennials in full sun unless the listing recommends another location such as shade or filtered light.

Acanthus
Spikes of white, lilac, or rose flowers on 4-foot stems. Dark green, 3-foot-long leaves. Takes shade, blooms in summer.

Agapanthus
Round clusters of blue or white flowers on tall stems above clumps of strap-shaped leaves. Blooms in summer.

Alyssum saxatile
Dense golden yellow flowers on 8 to 12-inch-high gray foliage. Plant as border or bulb cover. Blooms spring, summer.

Anemone (Japanese)
Semi-double white, pink, or rose flowers; 2 to 4-foot-tall dark green foliage. Grows in partial shade, blooms in fall.

Arabis
White, pink, or rose-purple flowers on plants from 4 to 10 inches tall. Takes light shade, blooms in spring.

Asparagus fern
Tiny fragrant pinkish flowers. Foliage upright or sprawling to 3 feet or more. Takes light shade; summer bloom.

Aster frikartii
Lavender blue flowers on 2-foot stalks. Flowers are fragrant single blooms to 2½ inches wide. Blooms spring to fall.

Astilbe
Plumelike flowers in pink, white, on stems to 3 feet high. Leaves serrated. Takes sun, light shade. Blooms spring, summer.

Aubrieta
Rose, red, lilac, and purple flowers on low mat of foliage to 6 inches high, 18 inches wide. Plants bloom in spring.

Bergenia
Pink flowers on stalks 12 to 18 inches high; rounded glossy-leafed foliage. Plant in shade, blooms in winter or spring.

Bleeding heart
Pink and white, heart-shaped flowers hang from 2 to 3-foot arching stems. Best in shade garden. Blooms in spring.

Calceolaria
Yellow, red brown, or spotted flowers. Kinds from 8 inches to 6 feet tall. Plants bloom in spring and summer.

Campanula
Blue, white, or pink bell-shaped flowers. Many kinds from a few inches to several feet tall. Blooms in spring and summer.

Catharanthus roseus
White or pink flowers on glossy spreading foliage to 2 feet high. Loves hot desert climates. Blooms summer and fall.

Chamomile
Yellow and white, daisylike or button flowers. Fine leafed plants form mat from 3 to 12 inches high. Blooms spring to fall.

Chrysanthemum
Almost any color or shade except blue on plants from 3 to 5 feet tall when planted in the garden. Blooms summer to winter.

Columbine
Odd-shaped flowers in red and yellow, yellow, blues, and purples on plants from 1 to 4 feet tall. Spring blooming.

Coral bells
Pink, red, or white flowers on stalks to 2½ feet tall above low rosette of dark green leaves. Blooms April to August.

Coreopsis
Yellow orange flowers on long stalks. Six-inch-high mat of leaves. Remove faded flowers to prolong spring-to-fall bloom.

Daylily
Many shades of yellow, red, orange, cream, lilylike flowers on stems to 6 feet tall. Blooms from May into fall.

Delphinium
Tall blue, white, or pink flower spikes reach 8 feet. Flower stems need to be staked. Blooms in summer.

Dianthus
Carnations and relatives with pink, rose, red, yellow, orange flowers on stems to 4 feet tall. Blooms from spring to fall.

English daisy
White, red, or pink short-stemmed daisies on low rosettes of rounded leaves. Needs shade in hot areas. Spring bloom.

Fibrous begonia
White, pink, and red bloom massed above foliage from 4 inches to 18 inches. Needs light shade. Summer bloom.

Foxglove
Purple, yellow, pink, white flower spikes reach 8 feet tall above clumps of gray green leaves. Plant in shade for summer bloom.

Gaillardia
Yellow, bronze, scarlet daisylike flowers on tall stalks. Gray green foliage grows to 4 feet tall. Blooms from June until frost.

Gazania
Yellow, pink, orange, and white daisylike flowers on clumping or trailing foliage to 6 inches tall. Blooms spring and summer.

Geranium
Enormous variety of form and color in flowers and in leaves; are really forms of *Pelargonium.* Blooms summer, fall.

Gerbera
Yellow, orange, coral, flame, red; daisylike with fine petals on stems to 18 inches. Peak bloom is early summer and late fall.

Gloriosa daisy
Big yellow, orange, or brownish daisies reach 6 inches across; plants grow to 4 feet tall. Blooms in summer and fall.

Heliotrope
Violet, white, lavender clusters of blooms with strong scent on shrubby plants to 4 feet tall. Blooms in summer.

Hellebore
Greenish, purplish, white, and pink flowers among fan-shaped leaves. Grows to 3 feet. Winter, spring bloom; needs shade.

Hosta
Flower spikes above massed clumps of heart-shaped leaves to 2 feet high. Dies back in winter, resprouts. Needs shade.

Hunnemannia
Clear yellow poppylike flowers on 2 to 3-foot plants with divided blue-green leaves. Blooms from July to October.

Iberis
Whitish flowers on long stems above attractive dark green 12-inch foliage. Plant in fall or early spring. Spring blooming.

Kniphofia
Red and yellow cones of tubular flowers on tall stems above tall clump of foliage. Grows to 6 feet tall. Summer blooming.

Lily of the valley
Clusters of tiny, bell-shaped flowers on 8-inch stems above broad leaves. Needs cold winter. Spring blooming.

Limonium
Blue, purple, white, pink flowers are two-toned. Low, coarse foliage to about 1 foot tall. Spring and summer blooming.

Marguerite
White and yellow daisies (blue on *Felicia*). Plants are shrubby, rounded, to 4 feet tall. Blooms during warm season.

Matilija poppy
Huge white crinkled poppies with yellow centers on rangy gray green plants to 8 feet tall. Scented flowers. Summer blooming.

New Zealand flax
Huge 12-foot flower spikes above 6-foot clump of green or bronze strap-shaped leaves. Use as screen in mild climates.

Oriental poppy
Brilliant pastel flowers in reds, pinks, white on showy 4-foot plants with grayish foliage. Dies in summer, resprouts.

Pelargonium
Many flower forms and colors on woody, sprawling plants to 3 feet. Flower clusters are large. Spring and summer bloom.

Peony
Enormous red, white, or pink flowers on 4-foot plants with large leaves. Don't plant where winters are warm. Spring bloom.

Penstemon
Flowers in shades of pink, white grow on plants that reach 3 feet tall. Many native species grow in West. Spring blooming.

Phlox
Many flower colors, plant types in heights from 6 inches to 5 feet. Uses depend on size, growth habit. Blooms in summer.

Physostegia
White, lavender, and rose 10-inch flower spikes bloom on 3-foot stems. Will take partial shade. Blooms in summer.

Plumbago
Pale blue flowers on 6 to 8-foot branches that sprout from the ground. May freeze in winter; resprouts. Blooms in summer.

Primrose
Polyantha has solid colored or variegated flowers. Fairy primrose is pink or white. Grows to 6 inches. Blooms in spring.

Saxifrage
Many varieties with white, yellow, pink flowers bloom on creeping plants that do well in a rock garden. Summer bloom.

Sedum
Many varieties with yellow or pink flowers. Succulent leaves are erect or trailing. Many sizes. Blooms in spring, summer.

Shasta daisy
Big, white single or double daisies to 3 or 4 inches wide above dark, coarse foliage to 18 inches tall. Summer bloom.

Violet
Tiny and sometimes fragrant flowers in blue, purple or white. Leaves to 6 inches high. Needs shade. Spring bloom.

Yarrow
Yellow or white flowers in flat clusters on plants from 8 inches to several feet tall. Blooms in spring, early summer.

Taking care of perennials

Perennials include all those flowering plants that bloom year after year (with care) such as chrysanthemums, marguerites, or daylilies. Some perennials grow, bloom, and then die back to ground level each year, while others are evergreen and produce new foliage even when they are not blooming. Whatever their growth habit, perennials require some grooming during the year to keep them healthy and good looking. Some may need dividing or transplanting when they begin to look crowded.

Follow these four basic care techniques: *Shear* dead flowers from plants (like dianthus or marguerites) when the bloom season is nearly over. *Cut back* or remove woody or dying parts of plants (like geraniums or chrysanthemums). *Tip cut* to produce new sturdy young plants from old plants (like alyssum or sedums). *Break up or divide* to renew crowded masses of daylilies, coral bells, or Shasta daisies.

The illustrations and text on these two pages guide you through these four techniques. Selected plant lists are included with each technique. For a plant not listed, select the grooming technique best suited to the plant.

CUTTING BACK

On some plants the flower stalks can be cut back to a main stem or to ground level right after blooming. The sketch at left below illustrates how you cut plants like aster, chrysanthemum, delphinium, foxglove, gaillardia, gloriosa daisy, hellebore, iberis, penstemon, phlox, sedum, and yarrow.

For geraniums and pelargoniums, cut woody stalks back to a bud or sideshoot as shown in the center sketch below. Plants that produce new shoots from underground (like asparagus fern, fibrous-rooted begonia, or plumbago) can be cut back to ground level.

For polyantha primroses, cut off the top half of the old leaves after bloom to force a second bloom period (see sketch at right at bottom of page).

SHEARING

Use hedge shears or grass clippers to cut off faded blooms and not more than an inch of foliage. Leave as

MARGUERITE:
Shear blossoms when they fade

much leaf surface as possible since the plants may not sprout new growth from bare twigs. Shear such plants as alyssum, chamomile, dianthus, gazania, marguerite, phlox, rosemary, thyme, or any other evergreen with dense bloom.

MUMS: Cut old stalks to ground

LEGGY GERANIUM: Cut back to compact shape

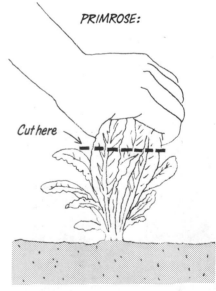

PRIMROSE:

Cut here

Cut old stalks *of chrysanthemums to ground level after bloom. New shoots will form at the base, flower next year.*

Cut back leggy geraniums *to a strong bud or sideshoot; new growth will sprout at cut. Trim from spring to fall.*

Cut off leaves *(half way) of polyantha primrose to produce a second bloom. Remaining leaves will have more light.*

TIP CUTTING

Many perennials quickly form new roots if you break off healthy shoots and stick the broken end into moist sand or prepared sand and soil mix (follow the techniques described on page 40). Some perennials that root easily are alyssum, arabis, aubrieta, bergenia, chrysanthemum, delphinium, dianthus, geranium, iberis, pelargonium, and sedum.

Remove healthy shoots *from crowded arabis. Have new pot filled with soil mix (see page 65) ready for cutting.*

Poke a hole *in soil mix large enough for each cutting. Once in place, gently firm soil around each cutting.*

Remove plants *when they have grown 2 inches. Good root growth looks like this. Replant to large container.*

DIVIDING

Some perennials form a dense clump with old growth at the center and young shoots around the edge. You can pry some clumps apart with spading forks (see sketch at left below), cut them with a knife or hatchet (see center sketch below), or dig them up and break off the young outside pieces (see sketch at right below) for replanting, then discard the old center piece. Plants that can be pried into sections are acanthus, agapanthus, daylily, and kniphofia (called 'red hot poker'). Plants with dense roots that need cutting apart are asparagus fern, columbine, iberis, Shasta daisy, and yarrow. Pull off rooted outside pieces of coral bells, chrysanthemum, and primrose for replanting and discard the woody center.

Use spading forks *to pry matted roots of daylily apart. Put separated clumps back in the ground immediately.*

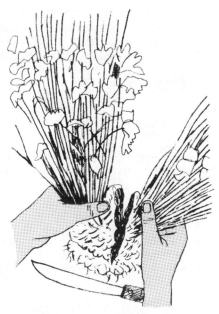

Slice dense roots *apart with sharp knife. Set individual clumps in the ground or in separate pots.*

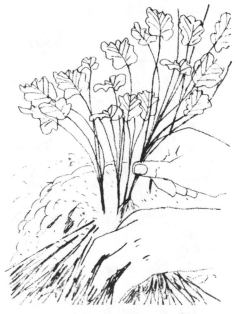

Pull apart roots *of young coral bells growing at outside edge of old clump that has been dug up. Replant, repot.*

BULBS
...a wide variety for seasonal color

The term "bulb" is often loosely translated to mean a number of unrelated kinds of plants. However, all these plants share a common characteristic: They store food in swollen underground parts during dormant seasons. When their growth season comes around, roots and leaves sprout from this natural storehouse.

Professional gardeners and nurserymen use several terms when speaking about bulbs, depending on how each plant forms its underground food storehouse. A true **bulb** (such as an onion, a daffodil, or a lily) is made up of fleshy underground leaves around a short piece of stem. A **corm** (gladiolus, for example) looks like a bulb, but the fleshy part is all stem. A **tuber** (such as some begonias produce) is also a piece of stem, but growth comes from several eyes or buds spaced over the surface. A **rhizome** is also a piece of stem, but has an elongated shape like an iris root, with new growth coming from the end. The swollen part of a dahlia is part of the root system, and is called a **tuberous root.**

True bulbs often bloom in spring, as do tulips, narcissus, and hyacinths, although lilies normally bloom in summer. Tulips and hyacinths grow well for only a season or two after you buy them, since professionals have given them special care (that you cannot duplicate) in order to develop big showy blooms. If you leave them in the ground, the flowers will get smaller and wilder looking the second year and may stop blooming completely.

Tulips and hyacinths require a period of cold weather in order to send them into complete dormancy before the growing season. Where winters are mild, buy the bulbs in early fall and store them in the vegetable bin of your refrigerator for a month before you put them in the ground.

Planting and care. Tulips, daffodils, and other spring bulbs look best planted in compact groups. (Don't set out long rows of plants unless you want them for cutting.) For a different and unusual planting effect, try tossing a handful of bulbs onto the planting area and planting each bulb where it falls.

Once the bulb has flowered, pick off the dead blooms but never cut the foliage. The bulb needs leaves to make food for the following year's growth and bloom. To camouflage the leaves until they wither and fall off, try planting fast-growing annuals over the bulbs.

	NAME	KIND, HARDINESS	FLOWER COLORS	PLANTING TIME	PLANTING DEPTH	SPACING; LOCATION	BLOOM SEASON
	Allium albopilusum	True bulb (hardy)	Lavender to lilac	Fall	2"	6-12". Sun	Late spring, early summer
	Anemone WINDFLOWER	Tuberous rootstock (hardy)	Blue, red, pink, white	Fall	1"	6". Sun, light shade	Spring
	Colchicum AUTUMN CROCUS	Corm (hardy)	Lavender to pink, purple, white	July–August	3-4"	4-6". Sun	Fall
	Crocus	Corm (hardy)	Yellow, orange, lavender, purple, white	Fall	2-3"	2-4". Sun, light shade	Fall to spring; depends on species
	Dahlia	Tuberous rootstock (tender)	Many (no blue)	Spring	See pages 108-109	3-4'. Sun	Late summer, fall
	Freesia	Corm (tender)	Many colors	Fall	2"	2-4". Sun	Spring

NAME	KIND, HARDINESS	FLOWER COLORS	PLANTING TIME	PLANTING DEPTH	SPACING; LOCATION	BLOOM SEASON
Galanthus SNOWDROP	True bulb (hardy)	White	Fall	3-4"	2-3". Sun, part shade	Spring
Gladiolus	Corm (tender to half-hardy)	Many colors and shades	Spring (winter in desert regions)	4"	4". Sun	Summer
Hippeastrum AMARYLLIS	True bulb (tender)	Red, pink, white, orange	Fall, winter	1"	2-4". Sun	Spring
Hyacinth	True bulb (hardy)	Red, pink, blue, purple, white, yellow	Sept.–Nov.	4-6"	6-8". Sun, light shade	Spring
Iris	Rhizome or bulb (many species hardy)	Many colors	July–Oct.	Bulbs: 4" Rhizomes: (See page 104)	Bulbs: 3-4" Rhizomes: 1'. Sun	Spring. Some varieties repeat bloom
Leucojum SNOWFLAKE	True bulb (hardy)	White	Fall	4"	6". Part shade	Winter, spring
Lily	True bulb (hardy)	Many colors	Fall	(See chart on page 33)	6-12". Sun or part shade	Summer
Lycoris SPIDER LILY	True bulb (tender or half-hardy)	Yellow, pink, rose, red	Late summer or fall	3-6" (in pots, expose tops)	4-6". Part shade	Late summer, fall
Muscari GRAPE HYACINTH	True bulb (hardy)	Blue, white	Fall	2"	2-4". Sun, light shade	Spring
Narcissus DAFFODIL, OTHERS	True bulb (hardy)	Yellow, orange, white, bicolors	Fall	3-6" (depends on size)	3-8". Sun, light shade	Late winter, spring
Nerine	True bulb (half hardy or tender)	Pink, rose, red	Aug.–Oct.	Upper half above soil in pot.	3 bulbs to a 6" pot. Sun	Late summer, early fall
Ornithogalum arabicum	True bulb (half-hardy)	White	Fall	2"	3-6". Sun	April-May
Ranunculus	Tuber (half-hardy)	Many colors (no blue)	Fall	2"	3-4". Sun	Spring
Tigridia	True bulb (tender to half-hardy)	Orange, pink, red, yellow, white	Spring	2-4"	4-8". Sun, light shade	July-August
Tuberous Begonia	Tuber (tender)	Many colors (no blue)	Winter, early spring	See pages 108-109	Grow in pots. Filtered sun	Summer to fall
Tulip	True bulb (hardy)	Many colors	Fall	4-6" (depends on size)	4-8". Sun, light shade	Spring
Zantedeschia CALLA LILY	Rhizome (tender to half-hardy)	White, gold, red, pink	Spring or fall	2-6" (depends on climate, variety)	1-2'. Sun or part shade	Spring, summer
Zephyranthes	True bulb (half-hardy)	Rose, pink, yellow, white	Spring (summer, fall in mild areas)	1-2"	3". Sun	Fall

Dividing bulbs

Bulbs have the same happy characteristic as perennials: You can start with a few and in a few years the number will have multiplied—that is if you know how to divide the plants. Some of the most common techniques are described below.

DAFFODILS

Daffodils and other members of the narcissus family can be left in the ground for several years and still bloom freely each season. To divide, dig up the plants when foliage has dried and yellowed. You'll find the mother bulb surrounded by several bulblets; remove only those which break away easily. Store and replant in fall.

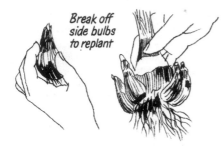

Break off side bulbs to replant

IRIS

Bearded iris and other plants which grow from rhizomes begin to show signs of being crowded every 3 years or so. Divide them in late summer or early fall. Lift out the root mass with a spading fork, then use a sharp knife to cut off the new rhizomes growing on the outer edge. Discard the rest.

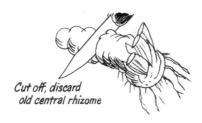

Cut off, discard old central rhizome

LILIES

When the lilies become crowded, dig them up in the fall. Then, to divide, remove a few outer scales and plant them shallowly in a loose, well drained soil. In a year they'll be full grown. Replant the old bulbs as well.

Break off a few outer lily scales—plant bulb and scales

DAHLIAS

When early winter frosts turn dahlia foliage brown, it's time to dig up the tubers and store them away. You can divide them before storing. Use a sharp knife and cut apart the new tubers so each has part of a crown attached to it and at least one dormant eye. Store them in dry sand or peat moss in a dry and cool place.

Each division must have bud here

GLADIOLUS

Gladiolus corms do best if they're dug up in fall and stored during winter. Do this after bloom season is well past and when leaves have turned a yellowish green.

Sometime you'll find that two large corms have developed. Break them apart. Otherwise, you may wish to increase them by cutting them into halves or thirds. Also, cormels (see sketch below) can be grown to full size in 2 or 3 years.

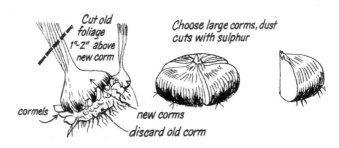

Cut old foliage 1"-2" above new corm

Choose large corms, dust cuts with sulphur

cormels

new corms

discard old corm

TUBEROUS BEGONIAS

When new shoots first appear on tuberous begonias you can cut them up to increase the number. Take good-sized tubers with 3 or more shoots and cut from top to bottom of the tuber between the shoots so each piece has a growing shoot. Dip cut surfaces in powdered charcoal or sulfur, and allow to dry for 3 or 4 days before planting.

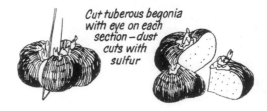

Cut tuberous begonia with eye on each section—dust cuts with sulfur

Planting bulbs

The planting chart below will help you set out the various kinds of bulbs that will bloom in spring (directions for planting other bulbs are given on pages 106–107). You'll need a ruler and a trowel or bulb planter.

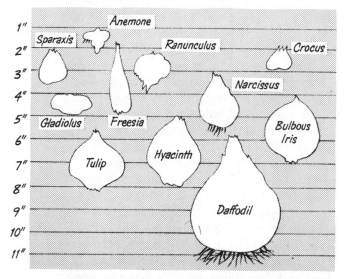

In September or October, dig a hole or trench about 3 inches deeper than the depth indicated on the chart. Mix a tablespoon of bone meal or superphosphate into the bottom soil of each planting hole, then cover with an inch of sand. Set the bulb in the hole and insert a short piece of bamboo beside it (be careful not to damage the bulb). The bamboo will act as a marker for each planting

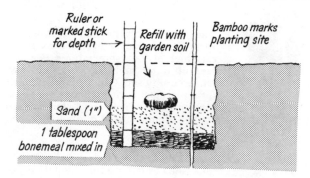

site. Then fill the hole with soil until level. Sow or plant spring annuals over the bulbs. They will fill in after the bulbs have flowered. Pansies, violas, or alyssum are good choices. If your soil is mainly clay, or if you plant in late fall, plant the bulbs about an inch shallower than the chart indicates.

TUBEROUS BEGONIAS

The easiest way to care for begonia tubers is to plant them in pots or small flats, even if you decide to bury the pots in a garden bed later on. Start the tubers in late winter in a mixture of leaf mold and peat moss. Cover with ½ inch of the mixture (be sure the eyes are on top of the tuber). Keep them indoors or in a greenhouse

(keeping the soil moist but not wet) until after frost. When the plants have 2 or 3 inches of growth, move them to an area that has early morning sun but is protected from mid-day heat (can have filtered sun).

DAHLIAS

After the last frost, you can set out dahlias (see sketch below), filling the planting hole as sprouts grow. Work a tablespoon of complete fertilizer into the bottom soil of the planting hole. A supporting stake is not necessary for small plants or small-flowered big plants, but is a must for kinds with giant flowers.

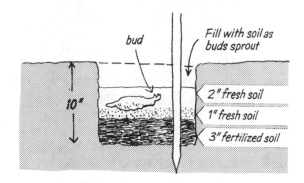

GLADIOLUS

If you want to grow gladiolus for cut flowers, then plant a few corms every two weeks beginning in mid-winter (in mild climates) or after the last frost (in cold climates). You can start cutting when the first blooms on a flower spike have opened. With the staggered plantings, you should have a continual supply of flowers for cutting.

Planted two weeks apart (right to left), gladioluses will provide cut flowers in spring and summer.

VEGETABLES
...home grown varieties have the best flavor

Most of the vegetables sold in markets and grown in vegetable gardens are well known. The last major introduction of new kinds of vegetables took place in the sixteenth century when Europeans began to arrive in the Western Hemisphere and returned to Europe carrying seeds of white potatoes, tomatoes, peppers, corn, squash, and climbing beans, together with such plants as tobacco and cocoa.

You don't need a big plot of ground to grow vegetables. Many of them are decorative and can be interplanted with your garden plants. Others are suitable for planting in containers. A special space-saving method of planting vegetables is described on page 115. And homegrown vegetables are often more flavorful than those from the market, since market varieties are chosen for their shipping qualities and are picked long before you buy and eat them.

Vegetables need all the water, nutrients, and sunlight you can give them. Before buying any vegetables, choose a planting site that gets full sun for most of the day. Then rough out a plan on paper of where each kind of plant will go. Prepare the soil as described on page 12 or 13, adding a complete fertilizer or well rotted manure and bone meal or superphosphate. Plant the seed or set out young nursery plants. When the plants are a couple of inches tall, cover the ground immediately around the plants with a mulch (see page 24) to conserve moisture and stop weed growth. Feed leafy vegetables with a nitrogen fertilizer once or twice during the time it takes for them to reach full growth. If pests become a problem, see pages 30 and 31 for control methods. Be sure that you never use an insecticide on vegetables that you plan to harvest within a week or so. Consult product labels for instructions on how long to wait between spraying and harvesting.

The edible leaves

Under this heading are two very easy-to-grow and good-tasting vegetables (Swiss chard and leaf lettuce), and two others so challenging to grow (spinach and celery) that 99 out of 100 gardeners would rather buy them at the store.

Spinach

You can sow seeds from July to September so it can grow to maturity during fall, winter, and spring (depending on your climate). Long daylight hours of late spring and summer heat make it go to seed too fast. Spinach requires a rich soil that drains well. When seedlings get a good start, thin plants so the remaining ones are 4 inches apart. In summer, you can grow an unrelated (but similarly flavored) plant called New Zealand spinach.

Swiss chard

Ideal for any vegetable garden (even as your only crop), easy to grow, pretty, and it yields continually through the first summer without going to seed. Grow it in any sunny spot—among flowers or whatever. Young seedlings transplant easily. Space plants at least 12 inches apart. Rhubarb chard has red stems, attractive leaves, and is valued for floral arranging. Its taste is slightly sweet. Rhubarb chard may develop a fat root like its close relative the beet.

Celery

Plant celery only if you're looking for a horticultural challenge. It doesn't tolerate very high or low temperatures, is a heavy user of water and nutrients, and needs sandy or silty soil. Can be planted in early spring in most regions. Seeds are slow to germinate, so it's best to start them indoors 2 months ahead of planting time.

All the lettuces

Illustrated at left are representative varieties of the four kinds of lettuce. From top to bottom: 1) crisphead or heading; 2) butterhead; 3) a kind known variously as leaf, bunching, loose leafed, or loosehead; and 4) romaine. Crisphead is the trickiest to grow because to achieve a perfect shape requires a constant temperature of between 50 and 60 degrees. If it's too hot, the central stalk elongates and loses quality. The other types of lettuce are easy to grow. Butterhead varieties are loosely folded with smooth yellow center leaves. Leaf lettuces are best for growing in a hot climate. Cut off leaves from outside the cluster as you need them. Plant rows of several different kinds of lettuce at intervals through the year to keep a continuous, varied supply coming on. Space leafy varieties 5 to 10 inches apart in the row, heading types 10 to 18 inches apart.

The cole crops

"Cole crops" is just another name for the cabbage family. A cole crop's two worst enemies are hot days (which make them go to seed) and aphids. Where summers are cool and rainy, these crops do fairly well. And, if your winter is not too severe, you can plant in August, September, or October so the plants will mature (about 90 to 150 days) during the cool season, which is also the aphids' off-season. Your best planting season locally for each of these crops is when the nurseries sell started plants. That, incidentally, is the best way for a beginning gardener to start any cole crop. Plant them in full sun. Water often; fertilize several times during growth period.

Cabbage

There are cabbage varieties that take 2 to 3 months to mature; these plants should be spaced 12 inches apart. Other varieties mature in 3 to 4 months and need to be spaced 18-inches apart. As plants grow, mound soil around stems to support the tops. Additional roots will grow from the covered stems. Pick cabbages when heads are round and firm. Try growing one cabbage in a small soy tub for a unique patio container plant.

Broccoli

This vegetable is very sensitive to heat, especially heat combined with good growing conditions. At first you might think it's growing mightily (which it is), but too suddenly you find that the heat has forced it to flower—which means it's too late for good eating. Pick broccoli while heads are tight. When heads start to spread, the skin on the stems will be thick and require peeling off. Pick off stems that you need from the base, leaving the less mature ones farther up the stem to develop.

Kale

Imaginative gardeners plant this vegetable in flower borders and in prominently displayed containers. Its pretty leaves (gray-green or blue-green) are curled and corrugated to the point that they look almost unreal. Cooked like spinach or shredded in salad, kale is delicious but strong in taste. Nurseries seldom sell started plants, so you'll most likely have to buy the seed and sow it. Plants are easy to transplant. Kale can be grown into summer more easily than other cole crops; it doesn't head and isn't as inclined to go to seed in hot weather.

Kohlrabi

Like kale, kohlrabi must be grown from seed. The eating part is the swollen stem section above ground; it's especially good sliced like a cucumber.

Brussels sprouts

Although many people tend to drop the final "s" in pronouncing the first name of this vegetable, the correct term is Brussels sprouts (it was named after the capital of Belgium). As plants begin to grow, support the stems by mounding soil around them. When the big leaves begin to turn yellow, it's time to start picking. Snap off the little sprouts from the bottom first—they're best when slightly smaller than a golf ball. Leave the little immature sprouts on the stem to develop. Brussels sprouts continue to produce over a long period; a single plant will yield from 50 to 100 sprouts.

Cauliflower

Of all the cole crops, cauliflower is the most difficult to grow successfully, but it is worth a try. It grows best in a cool, moist climate. Daily sprinkling is helpful, especially if a dry, hot spell comes along. The curd (the white part that you eat) doesn't form until toward the end of the growing period. When you see it, fold the outer leaves over the curd and tie them in place to protect it from sun.

The bulb crops

Bulb vegetables are easy to grow and they continue to grow for most of the year, constantly waiting to be harvested.

All the onions

Onions are especially easy to grow; they need only a fairly rich soil, and regular watering. Applications of fertilizer several times a year will make them grow faster. You can plant onion sets (baby onions from seed stores) all winter and up through April in mild climates; in harsh-winter climates, plant them in early spring. After three weeks, you can begin to pull them up, but they'll be white, moist, and perishable at this stage. Seeds need about 5 months to mature; sets need 3 to 4 months. After tops die back, pull the onion bulbs out of the ground and let them cure on the surface for several days. The dry onions can be stored safely for considerable periods of time.

Garlic

Seed stores and some mail order seed houses sell "mother" bulbs for planting. They will look like garlic bulbs from the grocery, only firmer. Break them up into cloves and plant them with bases downward, 1 to 2 inches deep and 2 to 3 inches apart in rows 12 inches apart. One or two dozen cloves will be plenty for an average crop. Culture is the same as for onions; harvest the same way as dry onions.

(Continued on next page)

Leeks

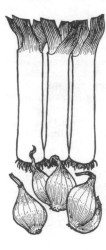

An onion relative, a leek doesn't form a bulb. Plant as seeds. As the plants grow, mound the soil around the fat, round stems to make the bottoms white, mild tasting.

Shallots

These mild, sweet onions are used in many gourmet recipes. They grow from sets like the dry onion. Plant in fall, placing each set 6 to 8 inches apart. Fertilize once or twice during the growing season. Dig up in spring. For white stems, ridge about 4 inches of soil up around the plants five weeks before harvest.

The vine crops

All vine crops originally came from the tropics and simply cannot stand a frost. Consequently, their growing season is limited to the time between the last frost and the first. In regions where there are only about four months between frosts, vine crop growers have to start early, often planting the seeds in paper cups or boxes a few weeks before the last frost date and then setting out the little seedlings when it's safe. To grow well, all vine crops need nutrients. Before planting, add a shovelful of manure to the soil in each planting site. Then plant the seeds. Remove weeds as they appear; water often.

Squashes and pumpkins

Two basic types of squash are summer and winter squash. **Summer squash** (such as scallop or zucchini) takes only about two months to ripen from seed. **Winter squashes** have hard shells; they need three or four months to ripen, as do **pumpkins**, a close cousin to the squash family. Plant seeds in late spring, when weather is beginning to warm up. Give plants plenty of room to grow; water often. To avoid rot, make sure ripening fruit rests on dry ground (see page 22).

Cucumbers

Owners of small gardens often have difficulty finding room for any of the vine crops because they need at least a 5 by 5-foot ground area. Because of their light weight, cucumbers adapt well to being trained up trellises, thereby saving space. Plant them 18 inches apart, train the center stem vertically up the trellis to the top, then pinch the top off and train the side branches sideways. Otherwise, grow in the same way as you would pumpkins, squash, and melons.

Melons

To ripen to full sweetness, melons need from 2½ to 4 months of heat. They will not tolerate foggy or cool summer days. You

grow melons in the same way as other vine crops; however, they can't develop the desired sweetness without the needed heat. Watermelons need more heat than other melons and more space than other vine crops (8 feet by 8 feet). Of all melons, cantaloupes are easiest to grow because they ripen the fastest.

The edible roots

The root crops listed here are not as closely related as you might think. Carrots and parsnips belong in the parsley family. Radishes and turnips are mustards. Salsify is one of the daisies or composites. Beets belong to the goosefoot family. Although different in most respects, all have certain requirements in common: Sow as early in spring as possible; they grow when it's cool and, generally speaking, heat can reduce their quality. Manure blended into the soil before planting makes them grow well, as does a thin band of commercial fertilizer placed 2 inches out from the row. Seeds are often slow to germinate; give them continual moisture to make them sprout and grow vigorously.

Beets

Plant a 10-foot row in spring (or fall where winter is mild), mulch lightly so soil won't crust, keep the bed moist, and in about 60 days it will yield 60 delicious, tender small beets (tenderest at 1½ to 2 inches in diameter). When foliage on plants reaches 5 inches high, begin pulling out excess so that by the time the remaining plants are 60 days old (harvest time) they will be 4 inches apart. The plants you removed (beets and tops) can be cooked and eaten.

Parsnips

These vegetables are related to the carrot, with culture quite similar, but growth much slower—four months from seed to harvest. In cold winter areas, it's best to sow seed in late spring, let the plants grow through summer, harvest in fall, and leave the excess in the ground to be dug up as needed all winter. In milder climates, parsnips will rot if left in the ground; sow seed in fall and harvest in spring. You must have deep, loose soil for parsnips. In heavy soil, sow seed in holes or trenches filled with sand or with ¾ sand and ¼ soil.

Radishes

You can harvest some kinds of radishes three weeks after you sow the seed. Speedy growth and relatively easy culture make this vegetable popular. They need continual moisture and some added nutrients to grow well. Supply the nutrients by blending rotted manure into the soil before planting or—about 10 days after planting—apply a fertilizer alongside the rows as for carrots, or feed with liquid fertilizer.

Carrots

Sow carrot seeds rather thickly (20 to 30 seeds per foot) because they germinate unevenly. Rocky or clay soil makes roots branch and grow crooked. Continual moisture and a non-crusted soil over the seed are needed to bring carrots up. When tops are 2 inches high, thin them out to leave 1½ inches between each plant and, at the same time, apply a thin band of commercial fertilizer 2 inches out from the row.

Turnips and rutabagas

Even if you don't like the taste of turnips, they are good to look at. Part of the fun of buying the vegetables is the choice of color and shape by variety. Colors are white, white topped with purple, and creamy yellow. Shapes are globular and flattened globular. Rutabaga is a tasty kind of turnip with large, yellowish roots. In cold winter areas, plant turnips or rutabagas in spring for early summer harvest or in July or August for fall harvest. In mild winter areas, grow as a winter crop by planting September through March.

Salsify

Salsify looks something like a parsnip and has a creamy white flesh that tastes a little like oysters. In fact, some people call it "oyster plant." Culture is much the same as for parsnips: Plant in a rich, deep, sandy soil which has been deeply tilled or spaded up. It takes 150 days for salsify to grow to maturity. Cooked, mashed, and mixed with butter and beaten egg, salsify can be made into patties and sautéed until brown to make mock oysters.

The lone cereal

As you might expect for a vegetable in the same family as bamboo and lawn grass, sweet corn has to be cared for in special ways if you are going to get a good crop. It must be planted after the soil has warmed and frosts are past. It must be planted in a series of parallel rows so that wind can distribute pollen effectively—otherwise few or no kernels form in the ears. It needs lots of water after growth starts, and especially at tasseling and after silking stages. It thrives on heat. After ears form, the kernels can go from the watery-kernel stage (immature) to the milky stage (just right) to the tough stage (too starchy to be good) in just a day. But if the weather is cool at ripening time, this progression may take a week. The sugar in picked corn changes to starch very fast, faster than field-to-market shipment, so there's nothing like the taste of sweet corn picked fresh and cooked immediately.

The perennials

Perennial vegetables grow tall and come back year after year. Plant roots in late winter or early spring. Some nurseries grow plants in cans so they're available all year.

Asparagus

Dig 12-inch trenches, work 6 inches of manure into the soil at the bottom and water thoroughly. Then wait two weeks before planting asparagus crowns. Set them 12 inches apart, gently spreading the roots apart. The crowns should be 6 inches below the top of the trench. Cover with 2 inches of soil; water well. As plants grow, add soil but never cover tips. Allow the plants to grow for a year before cutting off the spears.

Rhubarb

This vegetable is best planted in cooler sections, but you can grow it almost anywhere. Give it some shade in hot inland gardens. Plant at least 3 or 4 plants. Space the roots of each plant 2 to 4 feet apart, setting the bud top 4 inches deep. Water slowly and deeply. Let the plants grow through two seasons before harvesting. Be sure never to eat the leaves—they're poisonous.

Artichokes

Artichokes like cool weather, but can't take cold winters (they do best in the coastal belt of central California). Divide plants in early spring and plant with the base of new leafy shoots just above ground. Plants mature in about 18 months.

The potatoes

White (or Irish) potatoes are commonly grown in average-sized gardens, but sweet potatoes take up too much space for most gardens.

Yams and sweets

These vegetables are tropical and extremely tender. For summer growth in hot climates, they require rich and sandy soil and large growing spaces. Cut off and plant rooted shoots that grow from temporarily-planted tubers.

White potatoes

It takes a sandy, well-drained soil to grow white potatoes successfully. The subsoil should hold moisture well. Plant early in spring or in midwinter. Buy certified seed (they're perfect specimens) at a seed store and cut into chunky pieces (1½ inches square). Place the chunks (with eye facing up) 4 inches deep and 18 inches apart. Dig up early or new potatoes when tops begin to flower. Dig up mature potatoes after the tops die back.

(Continued on next page)

The solanaceous fruits

The solanaceous vegetables (or fruiting vegetables) have these traits in common: All are tender annuals and are widely sold as nursery plants in flats or pots at the right time for local planting. (You can also sow seed in flats about 6 weeks before the outdoor planting season.) Once these vegetables begin to produce fruits, they will continue to do so until frosts hit them.

Tomatoes

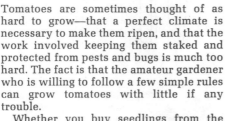

Tomatoes are sometimes thought of as hard to grow—that a perfect climate is necessary to make them ripen, and that the work involved keeping them staked and protected from pests and bugs is much too hard. The fact is that the amateur gardener who is willing to follow a few simple rules can grow tomatoes with little if any trouble.

Whether you buy seedlings from the nursery or plant seeds indoors following packet instructions, the ideal size for setting out plants is 2 to 3 inches tall. A dozen plants should supply enough tomatoes for any medium-sized family. Three to six plants may well be plenty. Plant seedlings at least 3 feet apart; dig holes deep enough to take all of the stems below the first leaves or branches—roots will form there. Some methods for planting and training tomatoes are illustrated on this page. The wire cylinder is particularly efficient, but you can use stakes or a flat rectangular support. Tomatoes left on the ground may rot before they ripen.

After the plants are settled, make a watering basin about a foot in diameter, enlarging it as the plant grows larger. Work a teaspoon of commercial fertilizer into the soil inside the basin. Water thoroughly. If cutworms are a local problem, put out bait immediately. Cultivate to keep weeds out but don't hoe too deep—roots are shallow. Feed according to fertilizer's label directions when immature fruits appear or after harvest.

Eggplant

This vegetable is slow and balky to grow from seed so you'd be wise to buy nursery plants. Set out plants at the same depth they grew in the flats (not deeper as with tomatoes). Shade young eggplants from sun for a week or so after planting.

Peppers

Pretty leaves, white flowers, and shining green or red peppers on 2 to 2½-foot plants make this vegetable very decorative. Plant in a sunny spot as you would a big annual or small shrub.

The legumes

Peas and beans are related in the botanical sense but have little else in common. Peas are a cool weather crop; beans require heat. Plant beans in late spring to mid-summer; plant peas in fall, winter, or early spring.

Peas and Chinese or snow peas

Plant in water-retentive but fast-draining soil. Add a little fertilizer when the plants are about 9 inches high. The edible pod or snow peas (commonly served in Chinese restaurants) are not stocked by most supermarkets. (They do not do well in warm-winter areas.)

Beans

This vegetable seed may not sprout if soil is too cold or too dense. Plant only when warm weather comes (April in many regions). Add amendments to heavy soil to make it workable. Pole beans, the kind you start twining up stakes or strings, mature 10 days to 2 weeks more slowly than bush beans, but yield more.

How to grow healthy tomatoes

Plant tomatoes deeply (you can bury half the stem). Space plants that will be staked 12 to 18 inches apart.

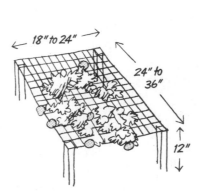
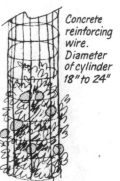

Use wire and stakes for support, and to prevent tomato plants from rotting on damp ground.

Intensive planting—an idea from France

The different approach to planting vegetables described on this page (called French intensive gardening) was introduced to the United States a number of years ago by Alan Chadwick of the University of California. It allows you to produce tender, flavorful vegetables in a minimum of space no matter what your original soil is like. This is what you do:

First, water the planting site deeply. A day or so later, dig up the soil and let it air for a few days more. Then, while the soil is airing, mark off rectangular planting beds 5 to 10 feet long and from 3 to 5 feet wide (you should be able to reach the middle without stretching). If you can, lay out the beds with the lengths running north and south so plants will receive the maximum amount of sunlight. Climbing crops like peas and beans need narrower beds (about 18 inches) for easy harvest.

When the soil is ready and the beds are marked, double dig the beds (instructions are on page 12) adding an organic amendment (such as manure or compost) and sand. The final mix should be two spade lengths deep and consist of about ⅓ organic material. Break up clods and remove any roots and rocks as you dig. When you finish the deep digging, evenly sprinkle a thin layer of bone meal and another of fireplace ash over the surface of the bed. Add 1 inch of manure or rich compost and fork it in to a depth of 3 to 6 inches. (Repeat this last step each time you plant a new crop.)

When you've finished digging, remove and set aside some of the prepared soil for use as a seed cover. The quantity you need varies with the kind of seed (see the package directions for recommended planting depth). Then rake the beds into flat-topped mounds about 4 inches high and water with a fine spray to moisten the upper layer. You can then sow the seed immediately; for transplants or nursery plants, wait a day.

Because they don't always transplant well, you must sow seed of the following vegetables: beans, beets, carrots, parsnips, peas, radishes, rutabagas, spinach, and turnips. Sow by tossing (broadcasting) the seed evenly over the whole bed, covering corners and edges as well. If you've never done this before, it might be wise to practice broadcasting by tossing rice onto a few sheets of newspaper until you can throw evenly. Most vegetables should be seeded heavily; then as the plants grow, thin them out gradually, so the soil is always shaded as much as possible by the leaves. For plants that take up little space, like carrots, the seed should be spaced about an inch apart. Seeds of larger plants, like bush beans, should be spaced about 5 inches apart. After sowing, cover the seeds with the soil you set aside earlier. Carefully spread it over the surface by shaking it from a shovel with a swiveling motion.

Transplants should be spaced in a staggered pattern as shown in the photograph of a lettuce bed at right below (lay a board across the bed to distribute your weight so you won't leave knee marks and foot prints). Each plant should be opposite an open space in the previously planted row. Distance between plants and rows should be a little less than the width of a mature plant. Leaf lettuce, for example, should be spaced about 8 inches apart. If you don't know how wide the mature plant will be, space the plants somewhat less than the distance suggested on a package of seed or in a garden manual.

The close spacing of both seeds and transplants allows the plants' leaves to act as a living mulch, shading the soil and keeping it cool and moist. You can assure good leaf cover and use your space more efficiently if you interplant quick growing vegetables between plants of slower kinds. For example, on a mound of cabbage plants you might sow radishes and leaf lettuce. The radishes and lettuce will grow to edible size while the cabbage is still rather small.

In watering the mounds of vegetables, try to keep the top layer of soil quite moist while the plants are tiny and offer little leaf cover. You may find that you have to water daily in hot weather. As leaves begin to spread, you can gradually cut down on the amount of water.

Spread manure *over layer of bone meal and ash on 4-inch-high mound of soil. Then, use fork to mix in amendments.*

Staggered rows *of leaf lettuce cover as much of bare soil as possible so root zone is kept moist and cool.*

TREES
...for shade, shelter, flowers, or fruit

Selecting a tree (like most garden plants) depends largely on what function you want it to perform. You may want its high, broad branches to form part of a wall, screening an unwanted view, cutting the force of the wind, or simply providing shade. Whatever your reason, you should study a tree's growth habits carefully before making a final choice. If you want a tree primarily for summer shade you should consider one that loses its leaves in winter, letting through sunlight on cold days. If you want a tree for a screen or windbreak, study the various types of evergreens whose foliage will protect you for the entire year.

Above all, don't fall prey to the impulse of many gardeners and choose a tree just because it brings back fond memories of another period in your life. For example, you may have happy memories of enjoying the shade under an elm, but, in your area, Dutch elm disease may be a problem.

CHOOSING YOUR TREE

Before choosing a tree, be sure to consider its ultimate height, and how long it will take to reach that height. Don't ever buy a tree thinking that you'll cut off the top if it grows too high; you will quite likely be very disappointed with the resulting shape.

Another point to consider is whether you should buy a tree that has a head start in growth or one that is still tiny. The type of tree will dictate what you should buy. For example, most fast growing trees should be planted when they are very young plants. If they remain in a nursery can too long, their roots may be severely damaged. (This principal does not apply to fully mature trees that are dug from the ground by tree movers and then replanted on your property, nor to large balled and burlapped trees that you can buy.)

LARGE SHADE TREES

Ideally, a large shade tree should permit a lawn beneath it, should give a high foliage canopy, and should provide some shade within 2 or 3 years after planting.

No matter what large tree you choose, don't expect it to be free of certain shortcomings. The professional may consider that the maple is too large for most gardens (it has a greedy root system), or that the ginkgo is too slow and erratic to grow. However, if you want one large, magnificent tree in your garden, an invasive root system may not be a prohibitive factor if you have the yard space to accommodate it.

MEDIUM OR SMALL SHADE TREES

Your choice of a medium or small shade tree should be dictated by the amount of litter it produces throughout the year, how much you can depend on its growth size, and whether you'll be able to walk under it without doing a lot of difficult pruning to get the headroom.

You can direct growth of the tree into the form you want by pinching out tips of branches at low levels. Remove lower branches in the third or fourth year when the head of the tree is large enough to take over growth.

TREES FOR SUN, WIND, AND PRIVACY

To achieve protection from sun or wind, or to provide a screen for privacy, choose a tree that has a low branching or weeping tendency. The wind screen should be 12 feet or higher; it will work best if it filters rather than blocks the wind. Many gardeners grow screen trees close together in a row, and top them at the desired height.

In mild climates of the West, medium-sized species of eucalyptus make exceptionally fine screen trees.

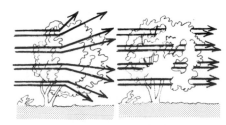

Dense branches *may break in wind. Thin to open holes.*

Never pile soil against a trunk. Make a well of planks

Buried trunk *may rot. Make a wooden well to let air in.*

Large shade trees (40 to 80 feet) . . .

MORAINE LOCUST	RED MAPLE	TULIP TREE	HOLLY OAK	SOUTHERN MAGNOLIA	GINKGO	RED OAK
Deciduous	Deciduous	Deciduous	Evergreen	Evergreen	Deciduous	Deciduous
Fast	Fast	Fast	Moderate	Moderate	Slow	Fast

Medium shade trees (20 to 50 feet) . . .

SWEETGUM	LITTLELEAF LINDEN	ARIZONA ASH	SILK TREE	WHITE BIRCH	WHITE MULBERRY
Deciduous	Deciduous	Deciduous	Deciduous	Deciduous	Deciduous
Moderate	Moderate	Moderate	Moderate	Moderate to fast	Slow

Small trees (15 to 30 feet) . . .

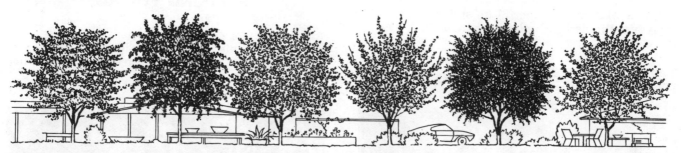

FLOWERING DOGWOOD	EVERGREEN PEAR	FLOWERING CRAB	FLOWERING CHERRY	OLIVE	EASTERN REDBUD
Deciduous	Evergreen	Deciduous	Deciduous	Evergreen	Deciduous
Slow to moderate	Moderate	Moderate to fast	Moderate to fast	Moderate	Moderate

Trees for screens (often topped at 20 to 30 feet) . . .

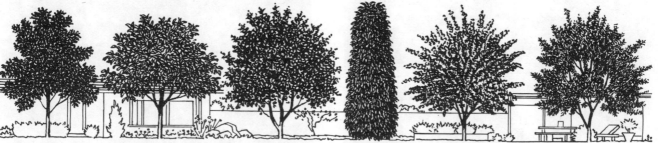

PITTOSPORUM	ENGLISH LAUREL	BUCKTHORN	LEYLAND CYPRESS	HAWTHORN	RUSSIAN OLIVE
Evergreen	Evergreen	Evergreen	Evergreen	Deciduous	Deciduous
Most kinds fast	Fast	Moderate	Fast	Slow to moderate	Moderate to fast

SHRUBS
...they come in all sizes, for all purposes

The term "shrub" is difficult to define because it can include anything from a dwarf rose to a towering mature holly bush, depending on placement and your treatment of it once it's planted. Generally, a shrub is thought of as any woody plant of small to medium-large size that usually has more ground-level foliage than a tree.

Two basic landscape uses for shrubs are as green walls of mixed foliage, or as single decorative plants that show off their flowers, fruit, or foliage.

The following lists contain only a selected few of the many shrubs available. In looking over these lists, keep in mind that just because a specific shrub is listed under a heading such as "Flowering Shrubs" or "Fruiting Shrubs" doesn't mean you won't find its foliage attractive. To make sure that any plant you choose is the right plant for your garden, ask your nurseryman for his opinion. Each listing is followed by letters which indicate that the shrub is deciduous (D) or evergreen (E).

FLOWERING SHRUBS

Spring: azalea (D or E); beauty bush (D); choisya (E); lilac (D); philadelphus (mock orange) (D); quince, flowering (D); rhododendron (E); rose (D); weigela (D).

Summer: abutilon (flowering maple) (D); buddleia (D); daubentonia (D); hibiscus (rose of Sharon) (D); hydrangea (D); hypericum (E); potentilla (D); rose (D); spiraea (D); viburnum (E and D).

Fall and winter: camellia (E) (to spring); daphne (E); forsythia (D); pieris (E); poinsettia (E or D).

FRUITING SHRUBS

Barberry (E and D); cotoneaster (E); dogwood (D); holly (E); huckleberry (E and D); kinnikinnick (E); lingonberry (E); Natal plum (E); Oregon grape (E); pyracantha (E); red chokeberry (D); skimmia (E); strawberry bush (E); toyon (E); viburnum (E and D).

STRIKING FOLIAGE

Aucuba (E); dogwood (small varieties) (D); fatsia (E); holly (E); mahonia (E); maple (small varieties) (D); nandina (E); oakleaf hydrangea (D); redbud (D); viburnum (some evergreen varieties) (E).

Forsythia flowers *offer splash of yellow across winter landscape. Cut them in tight bud for indoor display.*

Mock orange's *white flowers arch overhead in spring, perfume the garden with their strong fragrance.*

Giant clusters of rhododendron blossoms are called "trusses"; can sometimes completely hide foliage.

Tree-sized lilacs are very old. Most plants are smaller. Perfumed violet or white flowers bloom in spring.

Fatsia's bold leaves are its best feature, but it needs a mild climate to do well. Good against plain background.

Holly berries contrast with dark spiny foliage. To get berries you must have a female plant, and there must be a male plant nearby.

Choisya produces mass of white flower clusters in spring. Glossy, pale green leaves are attractive all year.

MAKING WORK EASIER
...how to deal with the big jobs

Most gardeners learn through hard experience how to make the occasional difficult and hard-to-manage chores as easy as possible. So that you, too, won't have to learn the hard way, study the helpful suggestions and illustrations given below and on the following two pages. Some of the suggestions are just common sense approaches. Others were carefully thought out and developed by long-time gardeners.

A general rule to keep in mind: If a gardening chore seems beyond your strength, then ask a friend or neighbor for a helping hand, or study the problem and try to come up with an easier approach. Serious accidents often happen when gardeners overtask their physical capabilities. Keep in mind that most chores are not so crucial that they can't wait until help is available.

LIFT WITH A STRAIGHT BACK

Whatever the weight of the object you are lifting, bend your knees and use your larger leg muscles as you lift. The bent-over, straight legged position that many inexperienced gardeners use to lift and move plants can strain the lower back muscles and leave you exhausted, if not in pain. Large objects should never be lifted. Instead, use a cart or dolly, or drag them on a piece of canvas or a wooden plank.

SAVE EFFORT WHEN HAULING TRASH

Instead of moving piles of grass, hedge trimmings, or leaves little by little, use a square of canvas or sailcloth and dump lightweight trash onto it as you work. When the carrying cloth has enough for you to carry easily,

gather the four corners to form a bundle and haul it away.

Big cardboard boxes like the kinds used to ship paper goods are often available at markets. Try using them for hauling large amounts of debris to the dump. Oversized plastic garbage bags (available in most markets) will also serve this purpose.

USE WHEELS WHERE YOU CAN

Although a wheelbarrow is considered to be a must in most gardens, there are other wheeled vehicles and devices that can lend a helping hand—some you may already have available.

If your gardening chores only require the use of a wheelbarrow, guard against letting it tip as you go around a curve. If it should tip to one side, let go and back away fast. A loaded wheelbarrow can give a tremendous twist that strains muscles, and the handles may gouge you as they go by. It's much better to reload than to hurt yourself.

A large, four-wheeled wagon is perfect for moving masonry blocks, and works well for hauling sacks, nursery flats, several potted plants, or other heavy objects.

A big, two-wheeled cart can be bought or made of lumber scraps. It's ideal for moving big bulky loads like prunings, leaves, or even a collection of odd-shaped spades, shovels, and picks, that require a bit more room than a wheelbarrow can provide.

A hand truck or dolly is a necessity if you'd like to move heavy containers here and there. It also helps with moving heavy bags of soil amendment. A wheeled platform can be a movable seat for ground level chores, or it can be just big enough to hold a pot.

USE A LEVER

A 2 by 4 or a steel fence post makes a good makeshift lever if you want to move a rock, lift a heavy plant out of a hole, or pry up a stubborn root system. For use at ground level, prop the lever on a rock as illustrated below, or use a log or wood block. At the edge of a hole, lay a board or beam under the lever to keep the earth from crumbling.

You can also use a lever to slide heavy objects into position. On soft ground, use boards under the object as runners.

MOVE THE LADDER OR USE TWO PLUS A PLANK

Leaning out from a ladder to reach a piece of fruit or to prune a branch is very dangerous. Even on a firm surface, the ladder may tip over and send you sprawling to the ground. If the ladder is on soft ground, your weight will probably cause the legs on one side to dig in and you may fall off. To test the firmness of the ground, climb up to the first or second ladder rung and lean your entire body weight first to one side, then to the other. If the ground is unsure, put planks of wood under each ladder leg. For jobs like trimming a high hedge, borrow a neighbor's ladder and slide a board through the second rung of your ladder and the borrowed ladder to make a wide platform.

USE THE INCLINED PLANE

You can use a few smooth boards to form a ramp for hauling plants into and out of a car. The same boards

can bridge a short flight of steps or form a gangway from ground level to the rim of a raised bed. Then instead of lifting a heavy bale of peat moss or a bag of sand, you just slide or roll it along the ramp. The same ramp with a block of wood or log supporting the center will make wheeling compost to the center of the pile easier.

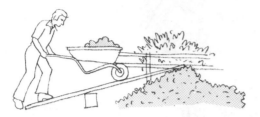

OVERCOMING FRICTION

The illustrations below show three ways to overcome friction when you want to shift heavy objects about. The easiest way is to simply slide a shovel blade under the object, then lift the handle and pull gently, but firmly. A smooth board will act as a runner when you want to pull a load across soil or grass, or move a heavy object across paving. Another technique is to use several lengths of thick dowel—as you push the plant container onto the last dowel, pick up the first dowel and place it in front. It helps to have a second person shifting dowels as you push.

CLEANING UP WITH WATER

To quickly remove leaves and other lightweight garden debris, attach any of the sweeper nozzles illustrated on page 20 to your garden hose. You can easily sweep off walks, patios, and driveways, then gather up the pile

and dispose of it. To avoid wasting water, always squirt toward a planting area that can benefit from a soaking, and keep the spray constantly moving from area to area.

REMOVING PLANTS FROM BIG CONTAINERS

If the container comes apart, this job is fairly simple. Even if you can remove only one side of the container, the plant will slide onto a dolly with ease and without lifting.

For solid containers, let the plant dry for a day or two, lay the container on its side (don't damage the plant), and tap the rim of the container firmly while pulling out on the base of the trunk. To make sure you don't damage the container rim while you work, cover it with a rag.

Another way to remove a plant from a container is to press your hose nozzle against the drain hole to float out the rootball. If the plant is rootbound, this will work well. If the plant is not densely rooted, you may wash away the soil ball.

A REALLY BIG DUST PAN

To move small piles of debris, cut a 5-gallon can as shown and file or bend the cut edges. Then punch holes in both sides about halfway between top and center and poke the ends of a length of rope through the holes and knot them inside. As an alternative handle, buy a strip of metal, bend it into a U-shape to fit the can, drill holes in the ends and the sides of the can, and attach to the can with bolts and washers.

GARDENERS' LANGUAGE
...a concise glossary of words you should know

The listing of gardening terms below is not limited to those terms used in this book. It also includes a number of other terms that a gardener should be familiar with so he can knowledgeably talk with nurserymen or other amateur gardeners. Because they are well defined within the book, a few terms are followed by a brief definition and page reference.

Actual (as in *actual* nitrogen). A term commonly used by farmers and soil scientists that is also useful in everyday gardening. It means the portion of a manufactured fertilizer (or any product containing several ingredients) that supplies a specific needed element. A 25-pound bag of fertilizer containing 22 percent nitrogen will yield 5½ pounds of actual nitrogen (25 pounds x .22 = 5.5 pounds).

Annual. A plant that completes its life cycle in a year or less. Seed germinates and the plant grows, blooms, sets seed, and dies—all in one growing season. Marigolds or zinnias are annuals. You may hear or read the expression "grown (or treated) as an annual." This means that you set out a plant after the last spring frost, then discard it when the first cold weather damages or kills it. The plant may normally live through more than one season in a milder climate.

Broad-leafed. Used in the phrase "broad-leafed evergreen," it means an evergreen plant with wide leaves instead of needlelike leaves. Used for weeds, it means any weed that is not a grass.

Bulb. Onionlike cluster of swollen underground leaves. See pages 106 and 109.

Cane. Normally used in speaking of the thick vertical stems produced by roses and such berries as blackberries and raspberries. Canes sprout from the ground, or from the base of the plant.

Chilling requirements. Many plants require certain amounts of cold weather in order to produce flowers and fruit, or even to leaf out properly. Some examples are cherries, lilacs, and peonies. If your winter climate is warm, ask your nurseryman for advice before planting such plants. Sometimes varieties exist that will grow well in warm areas.

Chlorosis. Yellowing of leaves caused by iron deficiency. See page 11.

Composite family (*Compositae*). Those plants whose flowers are daisy or asterlike. Each "petal" of a daisy is actually an entire tiny flower, called a ray flower. Other tiny flowers cluster to form the compact center of the bloom and are called disc flowers. Other examples of composites are chamomile, dahlias, marguerites, marigolds, and sunflowers. Chamomile is a composite that often produces only disc flowers in a buttonlike head.

Conifer. Plants such as juniper, cypress, fir, and pine that are sometimes called evergreens. Several are not evergreen, but all produce seeds in a conelike structure.

Corm. Swollen piece of underground stem. See page 106.

Crown. Portion of a plant at the joint of the root and stem or trunk. Sensitive to rotting if kept too moist.

Cultivate. To break up the soil surface around plants, removing weeds as you go. The resulting rough surface allows air to circulate and helps retain moisture.

Deciduous. Plants that lose their leaves for a season. On most plants and trees, the leaves die in late fall, but some desert plants drop them in summer to protect themselves from too much heat.

Double flower. A flower where the petals are numerous and clustered so that the center is covered by petals. Most hybrid roses are double.

Drainage. The term describes how water passes through the soil. The soil is well drained if water disappears from a filled planting hole in a few minutes. If water remains in the hole after an hour, the soil is poorly drained. The water itself does not damage the plants, but standing water drives out oxygen from the soil so roots may suffocate or be attacked by moisture loving organisms that cause rot.

Dust (noun or verb). A chemical product in the form of extremely fine powder, used to control insects or disease organisms. You apply by blowing the powder from a special applicator in windless weather. It forms a cloud that settles on the plant. Since it requires no mixing or water it is convenient to use; however, you never should try to apply it in windy weather.

Established. An established plant is one that is firmly rooted and is producing a good growth of leaves. But remember that an established container plant, such as one you buy from a nursery, must have time to reestablish itself after you transplant it.

Evergreen. A plant that never loses all of its leaves at the same time. Examples are pines, citrus, rhododendrons, and agapanthus. The term is often used as if it meant only the conifer.

Eye. Usually, the undeveloped buds on tubers which will sprout after the tuber is planted. Common potatoes have eyes in slight depressions over their surfaces. The word may also refer to any leaf bud which is completely undeveloped, such as those at the joints of a new hardwood cutting.

Flower parts. Parts are listed from the outermost cover to the center of the flower.

Bract. Modified leaflike structure that grows in a flower cluster or encircles a flower. Some are more striking than their flowers. The white cone of a calla is a bract.

Sepal. The outer circle of flower parts; for example, the green covering of a rosebud. Sepals may be colored as well as green. If they are united, the structure is called a calyx.

Petal. The second circle of flower parts. If petals are joined, the structure is called a corolla. The corolla may flare, as with petunias; or it may be bell or tube-shaped, as with various campanulas.

Segments. Lilies and tulips show no difference between sepals and petals, so both are called segments.

Spurs. Projections from the rear of the flowers, arising from either sepals or petals. Columbine has spurs.

Stamens. Parts of the central flower that produce pollen. Stamens are usually fragile stalks with pollen-covered swellings at the top. The stalks are filaments, the swellings anthers.

Pistil. The central part of the flower. It is often visible as a stalklike tube with a moist or sticky end. The tube is the style and the end is the stigma. At the stem end of the style is the ovary, the part that may produce seed and fruit.

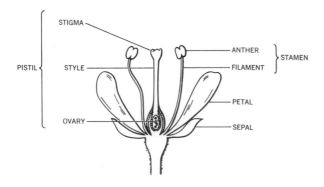

Forcing. Causing a plant to grow or bloom more rapidly or earlier than normal. Forcing may require extra heat, controlled light, or other special techniques.

Fronds. In the strictest sense, refers to the foliage of ferns, but the word is sometimes used to designate any foliage that looks fernlike, and also the featherlike leaves of many palms.

Hardy. In gardening terms, the word means resistant to damage by cold weather.

Heading back. A pruning term for cutting a branch back to a bud or side branch to change the direction of growth or force bushiness.

Heeling in. Temporary storage of certain plants by burying the roots in soil or sawdust. You might heel in bare root trees for a few days while waiting to plant; or you might lift bulbs while leaves are still green, then heel them in until the leaves die and you can store them.

Honeydew. A sticky, sweet substance produced by aphids and related insects. It may drip from trees, leaving sticky dirt on paving or cars underneath, and it sometimes supports the growth of a black fungus that spoils the looks of a plant.

Humus. Soft brown or black substance formed by vegetable matter in the last stages of decomposition.

Iron chelate (pronounced *key-late*). A compound containing iron in a form that plants can easily use. (See chlorosis, page 11.)

Leaching. Pouring water through soil to dissolve and carry away soluble minerals that might otherwise damage plants. To leach, water slowly for a long time, or set containers in water and let soak. Leaching will also wash away nitrogen compounds that plants need, so feed after leaching, not before.

Leaflet. Some leaves are divided into several small parts in a feather or fan pattern. Rose leaves are divided into from three to seven leaflets.

Loam. Soil (often dark colored) that is rich in organic material, does not compact easily, and drains well after watering.

Node. A joint along a plant stem where a leaf or branch may grow.

Organic. In gardening terms, organic refers to any material that was once alive, or that comes from a living creature. Sawdust, compost, bone meal, guano are organic, while perlite or ammonium sulfate are inorganic. In the term "organic gardening," organic refers to gardening without chemical sprays or manufactured fertilizers.

Perennial. A plant that lives more than two years, but usually not including large woody plants, called shrubs. However, some perennials are shrubby, while some shrubs are rather soft and fragile. In this borderline area, the term sub-shrub is sometimes used.

Pinching. Removing the tips of twigs and branches to force bushiness (see page 79). Called pinching because you use your thumb and forefinger rather than a tool.

Plant classification. Botanists (and other biologists) use a standard system for grouping and naming living creatures. This system of names can be useful to an amateur gardener, since a single common name often refers to a number of different plants. The terms below and on the next page are those most useful to a gardener, although only a part of the whole system of names.

Family. Every member of a family shares some characteristics, although individual plants may look quite different. In the rose family are such plants as cherries, pyracantha, roses, and strawberries. The lily family includes onions, tiger lilies, and yucca plants. Sometimes many members of the same family are prone to the same disease, even when they are externally different. They may also share cultural requirements.

Genus. The plural is *genera.* The first word in a botanical name is the genus to which the plant belongs, for example *Rosa, Prunus, Viola.* Occasionally this name is also the common name as with Anemone, Narcissus, or Sequoia.

Species. A genus often contains many close relatives, or species. A species is a single kind of plant, although there may be differences in appearance within a species.

Viola odorata is only the sweet violet, although it has a number of flower colors and forms. *Viola cornuta* is the viola, while *Viola tricolor* is the Johnny-jump-up.

Variety. A variety is some special form of a species. It is almost like other plants of its species, but may have a different flower or plant shape. *Viola tricolor hortensis* is the large flowered pansy.

Pollination. Pollen from flower stamens must be transferred to pistils for fruit and seeds to develop. This straightforward process is complicated for a home gardener by the fact that some plants have male and female flowers on separate individuals (holly), or separate male and female flowers on the same plant (cucumber), or mixed flowers with pollen that is useless on plants of the same variety (sweet cherries).

Rhizome. Swollen root of certain plants. See page 106.

Root bound. A plant is spoken of as root bound when it has remained in a container for so long that the roots grow around it in a circle. Seriously root bound plants are useless for planting in the garden since their roots will not grow normally. They may die or fail to grow, or blow over in the first good wind.

Rooting hormone. A powder containing growth hormones and sometimes certain vitamins. You dip the end of a cutting in rooting hormone before setting it in soil. The hormone stimulates root growth.

Single flower. Flowers with just a few petals are single (depending on their family the number varies). A single rose has five petals, a single poppy has four.

Sphagnum. A moss with long fibers sold dry for various garden uses. Use it for lining wire fern baskets, for air layering, or in chopped form as a soil conditioner. Much of the peat moss sold by nurseries contains sphagnum.

Standard. A plant that would normally grow as a bush with many branches, but has been trained by pinching and pruning to a single trunk. Roses are frequently grafted and trained as standards, and you may see azaleas, geraniums, or any other plant that is woody enough to support itself on a single stem.

Stolon. A stem that creeps along the surface of the ground, taking root at intervals and forming new plants where it roots. Another word for stolon is runner. Bermuda grass and strawberries form stolons.

Sucker. An unwanted shoot, often vigorous, that sprouts from the roots, base, stem, or even the main branches of a plant. Suckers often grow from rootstocks that have been grafted to a desired but weak-rooted plant. These are usually obvious because of a difference in foliage.

Taproot. Roots resembling carrots. Some plants that produce them are dandelions and oak trees. They often grow very deeply into the soil if there is a lack of water near the surface.

Tender. The opposite of hardy. That is, sensitive to cold weather.

Thinning out. In pruning, the term means removing entire branches, either large or small ones, to make a plant or tree less dense. In speaking of seedlings or young plants, thinning out means removing enough plants so that those remaining have room to spread leaves and roots.

Tuber. A swollen underground stem from which certain plants sprout. See page 106.

Photographers

INDEX